The Way of Discernment

Spiritual Practices for Decision Making

Elizabeth Liebert, SNJM

Westminster John Knox Press
LOUISVILLE • LONDON

Scripture quotations from the New Revised Standard Version of the Bible are copyright © 1989 by the Division of Christian Education of the National Council of the Churches of Christ in the U.S.A. and are used by permission.

Excerpts from *A Retreat with the Psalms,* by John C. Endres and Elizabeth Liebert. Copyright © 2001 by the Society of Jesus and the Sisters of the Holy Names. Paulist Press, Inc., New York/Mahwah, NJ. Reprinted by Paulist Press, Inc. www.paulistpress.com

The poem "Praying" from *Thirst* by Mary Oliver, copyright © 2006 by Mary Oliver, is reprinted by permission of Beacon Press, Boston.

Book design by Drew Stevens
Cover design by Night & Day Design

First edition
Published by Westminster John Knox Press
Louisville, Kentucky

This book is printed on acid-free paper that meets the American National Standards Institute Z39.48 standard. ∞

PRINTED IN THE UNITED STATES OF AMERICA

08 09 10 11 12 13 14 15 16 17 — 10 9 8 7 6 5 4 3 2 1

Library of Congress Cataloging-in-Publication Data
Liebert, Elizabeth.
    The way of discernment : spiritual practices for decision making / Elizabeth Liebert.—
1st ed.
        p. cm.
    Includes index.
    ISBN-13: 978-0-664-22870-5 (alk. paper)   1. Decision making—Religious aspects—
Christianity.   2. Spiritual life—Christianity.   I. Title.
    BV4509.5.L54 2008
    248.4—dc22
                                                                            2007051867

Contents

Practices

Acknowledgments

The genesis of this book lies in my own discernment processes over many years. I am grateful to my friends, religious superiors, and, especially, spiritual directors, who have carefully listened to and facilitated these discernments. The other taproot of this book is a workshop on discernment offered at First Presbyterian Church, San Rafael, California, which my associate, the Reverend Katharine Collette, arranged for—and for which I then had to develop the content and processes. This first workshop set the pattern for dozens of other workshops and retreats in churches, retreat centers, and classrooms. The many participants in these discernment retreats generously shared their experiences not only with their fellow participants, but also kept teaching me about how infinitely rich and creative God is in the ways God calls us as individuals and communities. I trust my facilitating helped these participants, and I gratefully acknowledge that their sharing has deeply enriched this book. My own spiritual directees, too, entrust me with their discernment processes, allowing me to follow the fruits of their discernment over time as it spreads through their lives. It is an honor to accompany you, and I continually learn again to trust that God will work through our human processes to bring freedom and fruit to our all-too-fallible choices. My editor, Stephanie Egnotovich, while "just doing her job," understood my task and audience so well that her suggestions were unfailingly helpful in moving from the inductive process used in the retreats to a form that makes sense to those of you who will experience this process only through the pages of this book. John Endres, SJ, graciously made room amid his own writing to comment on the biblical sections of this book. The staff at Villa Maria del Mar, Santa Cruz, California, gave me a quiet corner room in which I finished the final editing. Thank you to all. Finally, I dedicate this book to Christine, Margaret, and John, all of whom are engaged in potentially life-changing discernments.

Introduction

How are we to live our lives thoughtfully and faithfully in the midst of all the forces, options, and decisions that characterize modern life? Discernment, the Christian practice of seeking God's call in the midst of the decisions that mark one's life, may very well be the single most important Christian spiritual practice for dealing with this contemporary dilemma. We all make decisions constantly, some with careful reflection, many offhandedly and without much thought. What if we understood these decisions, minor as well as major, as a matter of faithful Christian living? Though many Christians do create their own practices of faithful decision making, most are unaware that a long and varied Christian tradition of discernment exists precisely to help integrate decisions into the life of faith. Learning some of this tradition, but more importantly, internalizing some of these practices and incorporating them into one's decision making: these are the goals of the journey you are about to undertake.

Henri Nouwen once remarked, recalling the well-known aphorism, "Nature abhors a vacuum," that one of the things preventing Christians from moving ahead in their spiritual lives is a fear of empty space. They need a set of boundaries to provide a container within which they can be emptied of themselves and filled with God.[1] My own experience teaching spirituality suggests that Nouwen was correct. Even when Christians recognize that such a thing as Christian discernment exists, they often still founder for lack of simple parameters. How do I begin? What steps do I go through? How do I know if I am actually discerning? This book seeks to provide a set of boundaries, a kind of container to assist you not only in understanding what Christian discernment is, but more importantly, in taking steps to becoming a more discerning person.

As we shall see in chapter 1, the fundamental meaning of discernment is discrimination. This book focuses on faithful discrimination in service of decision making. Before we can discriminate, however, we have to notice—both outside and inside ourselves, both circumstances and our inner responses. Then we have to make judgments about what is more conducive to our spiritual life and then to judge that *this* thing is better than that one, *this* action is better than other options for achieving that goal. But what provides the basis for such discriminations? Is it only what we can figure out for ourselves? Is it what feels good? Is it what makes me happy? Or what makes others happy? If we have to struggle, is it a sign that God doesn't want us to go in this direction? These are the very real questions that arise when people begin to ask seriously, "What does God desire here?" Finally, we have to choose: this thing over that one, this action over that one. Entering into discernment, then, means becoming increasingly able to notice where God is at work in the world and in one's own life, increasingly desirous of choosing the "more," and, God willing, increasingly generous with one's own life in response.

Important as it may be to come to a sense of what God might desire in the moment of decision, a still deeper benefit comes by engaging in discernment. The more one discerns, the more likely it is that one will become a discerning person. By the phrase "discerning person," I mean a person who seeks, in all that he or she does, that which better responds to God's call in the moment. A discerning person begins to desire what God desires more than any other created reality. Over time, and with God's grace, you can indeed become a discerning person. If this book succeeds, your former way of decision making will gradually be replaced by a discerning attitude. Your life will begin to take on a different orientation. You will be seeking God in places and through decisions that never occurred to you before.

When I first offered a church retreat on discernment to a mainline Protestant church more than fifteen years ago, one parishioner asked, "What is discernment? Is it New Age?" That this question surfaced in this well-educated congregation indicates how invisible this ancient Christian practice remains, especially among Protestants. This book seeks to change such perceptions. I will describe discernment—for until we know it exists, we are unable to choose to discern for ourselves. I will place it within the long Christian tradition—for if we are worried that it is somehow unorthodox, we will be unable to trust it to assist us to grow closer to God. But my central task is to invite you to actually do discernment—for unless we experience it for ourselves, we will miss the opportunity for spiritual depth that discernment can bring to our ever more complex and fast-paced lives.

The book unfolds in two parts. Part 1 sets out the biblical, theological, and historical context for discernment. The first chapter looks at what discernment is and where we find it in Scripture. We examine our notion of God and of human beings: Can God communicate with us? How do we hear? What is our part in discernment, and what is God's part? You will also begin doing discernment through the Awareness Examen, a simple daily practice that centers on noticing where God is active in one's daily life. Over time, the fruits of the Awareness Examen include a deepened ability to notice, desire, and choose God in the everydayness of our lives—those very places we often overlook as important for discernment. In the second chapter, we discuss spiritual freedom, the essential disposition for discernment. Here you will begin to seek this disposition, which always comes to us as God's free gift. As it takes root, its fruit appears as a growing desire to put God's call first in one's life. We then examine the role that desires play in discernment. The accompanying practice will help you to examine your own heart's desire. We also look a bit at our own spiritual histories in order to develop a clearer sense of how God has already been at work in our lives. All these practices and their accompanying discoveries are foundational to living a discerning life.

Part 2 is the core of the book, and I move here from introducing discernment in general to inviting you to practice it in concrete instances. At this point, I invite you to begin your own discernment process, rather than just thinking about discernment. This invitation is crucial. Accepting it will make the difference between understanding about discernment and experiencing discernment, between secondhand knowing about it to knowing for yourself. Practicing discernment experimentally will help you adapt the tradition of discernment to your own life and to begin to become a discerning person. In discerning about your own issues, as God leads you, you will meet God in and through your own life.

The first step in discernment involves formulating the issue for discernment. Chapter 3 assists in that process, for process it often is. Your issue will need to be sufficiently limited that you can get around it, sufficiently concrete that you can imagine and try on various possibilities in your imagination, and sufficiently focused that you know what you are discerning. The first practice is, then, framing the matter for discernment. It seems like a simple task. However, the central issue for discernment may be hiding inside of another, more readily apparent issue, only revealed as you jump into your discernment. Or perhaps, in gathering information relevant to the decision you are discerning, some piece of data comes to light that changes your issue substantially. The goal of chapter 3 is to frame your discernment with sufficient boundaries and clarity that you can work with it in the subsequent chapters, but to hold it with sufficient tentativeness that you can let it shift as you progress through the various exercises, always open to God's call for you through this decision. The remainder of the chapter, with its attendant practice, will help you begin to surface information and make some judgments about which information is relevant to your discernment.

Chapters 4–10 lead you deeper into your own discernment journey by means of a series of practices set in the form of prayer. Since one can move into making a decision from a variety of leaping-off points, so too discernment has a variety of starting points. Chapters 4–10 each use a different starting or entry point to lead you deeper into your discernment. These chapters focus, in turn, on memory, intuition, body, imagination, reason, a particular set of feelings called "religious affections," and nature. Why these entry points? If we observe the decision making of a large number of people, we soon discover that they rely on a wide variety of favorite strategies and techniques to decide an issue. Some make lists and quite literally think their way to a logical decision. Others recognize a decision in their bodies; they might say, "I know in my gut that this is the right thing to do." Others come to clarity by taking a long afternoon out in nature, sitting by the ocean or hiking in the hills. I myself rely on imagining myself into various possibilities, noticing what happens in me when I try on various options. Some people have honed their intuition to a fine point; they seem to arrive at a decision without going through separate steps—as if the solution just appeared whole. Some return to their storehouse of memories and find a comparable decision and use this memory to point the way. Still others compare their options to their deeply held values and see what option most closely expresses these values. Our ancestors in the faith were not so different from us. They too employed similar strategies in their attempts to understand what God might be calling them to be and do.

The first practices in chapters 4–10, the lead practices, are based on just such variations in preference and personality. Each chapter also contains one or more other practices that can enhance and deepen either the entry point as a whole or the lead practice. Should you attempt all the practices? Not necessarily. I have designed each chapter around the lead practice, however, and praying it will continue unfolding your discernment. Use the chapter's second or third practice to the extent that you feel called to them and they help you with your discernment. In a subsequent discernment, some of these other exercises may prove very useful. In any case, their variety reveals the richness of the Christian tradition of discernment.

In discernment, even after gaining a sense of the best decision for the moment, your discernment is not yet finished. The final step is confirmation, which is one of the distinctive aspects of Christian spiritual discernment. Figuratively speaking, we lay our discernment at God's feet. We bring to God the results of all our prayer and reflection, our tentative decision, our best effort to gain clarity. We seek confirmation of two kinds. First, is the tentative decision confirmed within us? Second, does it hold up when we examine it in light of the wisdom of the Christian tradition? In the final chapter, you will learn what some of this wisdom suggests and test your own tentative decision.

PERSONAL PERSPECTIVES

Who am I, and why did I want to write this book? The facts are easy to relate. I am a white, lifelong Roman Catholic religious Sister who teaches spirituality at a Presbyterian seminary set within a large ecumenical and interfaith consortium of theological schools. But what is harder to relate is how these facts came to be: my typical pre–Vatican II upbringing, the excitement of Vatican II that corresponded with my early days in my religious congregation, my struggles to learn to teach junior high–level math and science, my discovery that pastoral ministry could have many faces beyond teaching, my return to graduate school in religious studies and transition to teaching college religious studies while simultaneously working in the formation of new members of my religious congregation, my second stint at graduate school for a doctoral degree in religion and personality studies, and my subsequent move to seminary teaching.

But still that doesn't tell you about the struggles that have formed my person—the failures, the closed doors, the deaths, the boredom, and the hard work that have fueled my desire to understand discernment and incorporate it into my life. "What is it, God, that you want here?" has been my steady refrain for the past forty years. Still, my discernments have been my own; your discernments will be yours. You are a different person, and God is calling you personally and uniquely. My task is to help you listen, notice, discriminate, and choose within your own relationship to the One who ultimately sustains the whole world.

I am also a Christian who is writing primarily for persons within the Christian tradition. However, the practices, suitably adapted, may be useful to persons in other traditions or no specific tradition. I have, for example, occasionally used the exercises in situations where it is not appropriate to advocate a specific tradition. Yet discernment arose within the Christian spiritual tradition, and its fullest expression, I believe, assumes its practitioners follow this tradition.

I have a certain group in mind as I write. Given that we all make decisions, this book is for all serious Christians who desire that their decisions be a central part of the way they seek and respond to God. You need not have it all together to begin. All that is necessary is the desire to listen for God's call in the midst of your life. That is enough. We bring our little drop of generosity, and God responds. We ask for spiritual freedom, and God assists us to grow in it. We seek what is better in a particular situation, and God meets us in that seeking.

You will meet real people in these pages. No actual names appear. I have also altered details to protect identities.

Two disclaimers are in order about language for God used in this book. First, our language is more or less welcoming of persons who differ from us. Women, among others, have frequently felt unwelcome or invisible in church-speak. Therefore, I have tried to use gender-inclusive language for people and to avoid pronouns—inescapably gendered—for God.

Second, I am thoroughly Trinitarian in my theological beliefs. This book is intended to reflect and foster Trinitarian perspectives. But where one person might use the language of "Father" quite comfortably, another finds it a barrier, subtle or not so subtle, to prayer and discernment. When one person readily thinks of Christ as the active agent in his or her prayer and life, another more easily uses the language of the Holy Spirit. In the Fourth Gospel, Jesus tells us to wait for the Counselor who will bring to mind all that he has said and done and who will, in fact, teach us what we could not yet understand, so both of these prayers are standing on traditional ground in their prayer. Because I do not know the language for God you prefer to use as you pray, I generally use the more general term "God" in practices and explanations. I mean this term to stand in for the preferred language of address to God that each of you might choose to bring to the exercises. If you prefer, for example, to call on the Holy Spirit as you begin each spiritual practice, please do. You have a long Christian tradition behind you. If "Father" or "Creator" or "Lord" or "Christ" or "Jesus" are more useful to you or feel more personal, by all means shift the language. Our God is the one whom Jesus called Father; whom the Scriptures address as Creator and Lord of all that is; and whose Spirit, flowing from Father and Son, animates our lives and renews the face of the earth.

HOW TO USE THIS BOOK

This book differs in one essential dimension from the many good books on discernment that have appeared in recent years. You will not simply be reading about discernment; you will learn discernment through its practice. Since this method of proceeding asks unexpected things of readers, some advice will assist you to make the most of the information and exercises.

First, think of this book as a personal retreat facilitator. A human retreat facilitator would make suggestions for prayer or other activities and then talk with you about your experience, and I have set up this book to echo this dynamic. Each chapter begins with a practice, with enough detail so that you can launch into it for yourself. Once you complete your reflection, pick up the text that follows. The subsequent discussion adds commentary and connects the practice to the Christian discernment tradition.

Second, do the practices wholeheartedly. The practices at the beginning of each chapter, the lead prayer exercises, are the heart of the book. The words surrounding the practices are there simply to help you understand how to proceed and how to interpret what you experience. I encourage you also to try the supplementary practices, especially if you are new to discernment. They will enhance your discernment and give you a sense of the breadth of the Christian tradition of discernment.

Be sure to keep in a spiritual journal a record of your unfolding discernment. Each discernment exercise will generate thoughts, feelings, judgments, questions, all rich data relevant to your overall process and direction. In order not to lose the freshness and detail of your experiences, write down a summary of the insights and feelings that occur along the way. This rich life palette will then be available to weave back into the tapestry of your discernment. By reserving the same journal for all your discernment practices, you will soon begin to recognize patterns in yourself and in the way God calls you. You may also discover key metaphors and multivalent images that will lead you to further insight and reflection about the course of your life.

Third, since discernment is deepened in community, seek someone with whom you can share your discernment process. Ideally, you will have a friend, a spouse, a pastor, or a spiritual director who can provide this attentive presence. This person represents the larger Christian community, supporting your prayer and pondering. As you speak aloud about your experience, your discernment deepens. Perhaps, as I shall describe below, you can participate in a discernment group in which all the members listen and support each other.

Fourth, begin each exercise by asking to grow in the spiritual freedom upon which discernment rests. The first step in each practice suggests a form of this crucial preparation. Be generous with your time and yourself at this point. Resist the impulse to "get to the discernment"; this *is* the discernment. If you are unable to come to some measure of spiritual freedom, at least ask for a deeper desire for spiritual freedom. As you proceed with the reflection, you may feel your spiritual freedom ebbing away. Stop and renew again your desire to grow in spiritual freedom. Chapter 2 discusses this important foundation in more detail; the accompanying exercise will help you get started.

Fifth, take your time. You cannot push water up the river. Neither can you make clarity come before its time, nor make the Holy Spirit act on your command. Discernment is more than a means to a particular decision; it is a way of life. Sometimes, though, a decision is urgent. If you must make a decision quickly, do as much reflection and prayer as you reasonably can, make the decision that best grows out of your wisdom at that moment, and trust that God will be with you.

Sixth, assume control of your own discernment process. If a component of a practice or an entire practice causes undue anxiety, feel free to stop. Examine, perhaps with a spiritual director or pastor, what other issues might have been triggered or what might lie behind your response. If this kind of reflection also makes you anxious or resistant, then simply stop. You can move on to a different step or to the next practice. Likewise, when you are sharing with your friend, spouse, spiritual director, or prayer group, judge the content and level of self-revelation that feels safe yet simultaneously challenging. Do not violate your own sense of safety. If this topic is important for your growth, the Holy Spirit will prepare you to deal with it in more depth in the future.

Also, feel free to adapt the practices in this book to your individual or group circumstances. They have been constructed with a variety of persons and circumstances in mind, but their particular wording and focus may feel constraining to you. Feel free to adjust the language, including the language for God, so that the process better fits you or the matter you are discerning. Furthermore, though the tradition reveals that many processes have been employed in discernment, the essence of discernment lies in the prayerful searching for God's call, weighing and deciding on the most appropriate response. Any process that encourages such prayerful searching, weighing, and deciding might therefore appropriately be used for discernment. And never forget that the Holy Spirit can work outside the parameters of even the most carefully crafted process. While the practices contained in this book have been used fruitfully over a number of years, there is nothing particularly sacred in them.

You will likely find that some practices are more sympathetic to the way you naturally process information. I encourage you to notice your preference for certain practices, and build them into your personal discernment repertoire. At the same time, be aware that no single process provides a sufficiently complex means of uncovering all that you might need or want to know as you seek God's preferred future. Thus, I also recommend you regularly use at least one practice that offers very different data or relies on your less preferred ways of being in the world, for it may reveal some otherwise inaccessible information that may deeply affect your ultimate decision. For example, I rely heavily on imagination for my discernment. I imagine possible scenarios and then try them on for fit—that is, how they feel in my emotions and my body. Thus, I would naturally employ the practices based on imagination, feelings, and body. To balance this preference, I will frequently list all the pros and cons of a course of action and systematically think through the alternatives. Combining a more intellectual practice with the emotional and physical that I instinctively prefer lessens the possibility that my feelings and imagination might become disconnected from the concrete particulars and the realistic possibilities of a situation.

Finally, believe that God accompanies you wherever your decisions take you. In this sense, you cannot fail discernment. A poor choice may not necessarily be a bad discernment, because discernment is not measured by outcomes but by our increasing sensitivity to God's gracious invitations and desires for our welfare. The only ways we can fail at discernment are by stubbornly turning our back on spiritual freedom or by deciding not to seek God's call in this situation at all. Even then, God remains with us.

USING THIS BOOK IN GROUP SETTINGS

An ideal way to use this book the first time is in the context of a discernment group. Discernment concerns call, and call is best uncovered in the context of community. This book can be used in two kinds of groups. In the first, each person works with her or his own discernment, but shares from the fruit of prayer and reflection at each group meeting. This kind of group provides an excellent setting in which to learn discernment because part of the group's time together can be given to discussing the content of each chapter. In addition, the faith sharing, magnified as it is by the attention and contribution of all the members, can bring enormous support for each individual's personal discernment, and a sense that every person's discernment will be unique.

In the second kind of group, the group members focus on one person at a time, taking turns supporting each other's discernment from start to finish. This option makes the most sense for long-term sharing or discernment groups, which have the leisure to attend to each person for as long as necessary to complete the discernment. Those members not presently engaged in a discernment process simply support by prayer and contemplative listening the member who is, knowing that at another moment others will return the support. The first kind of group may evolve into the second, after completing their introductory study, or if they choose to reconvene whenever a member desires support for a new discernment. The advice below concerns the first of these variations.

First, choose the number of meetings to balance the way the book is constructed and the needs of the group. The most straightforward option is to proceed at the rate of one chapter per week for an eleven-week commitment. Adjustments to this length of time should preserve the sharing at the heart of each chapter in part 2; to give sufficient time for that personal sharing, I recommend at least one week per chapter in part 2.

Second, choose the appropriate size for your group. Groups of between four and seven are ideal; groups of more than seven participants should break into smaller groups of four to seven. It's best if these small groups remain constant for the duration of the study. Dividing the groups by compatibility is not necessary; in fact, the more diverse the group, the better. Spouses can decide if they would feel freer in the same or in separate groups.

Third, select leadership. The leadership can easily rotate, or one person may assume leadership for the study in part 1 and another for the sharing in part 2. In this case, select these two leaders by the different skills needed for each section. For part 1, the ideal leader will be able to summarize the main content points and to help others remain on track in a discussion of the main ideas. For part 2, the skills of helping people be comfortable with silence, inviting sharing, and creating an atmosphere free of intrusive advice giving rise to the fore. Since the leaders serve primarily as process facilitators, they can engage in their own discernment along with the other members.

Fourth, covenant together. The group process and the individual discernment of each participant benefit if everyone makes five commitments.

1. Commit to the entire process in order to allow sufficient trust to build in each person and in the group as a whole.
2. Contribute actively from your own prayer and reflection, but maintain the boundaries and level of vulnerability that, for you, are appropriate and safe.
3. In order to allow time for all group members, limit your sharing accordingly.
4. Avoid offering advice or telling another, however subtly, what to do, since advice giving can easily intrude negatively upon another's discernment process.
5. Keep everything that is shared in the group strictly confidential.

Fifth, practice contemplative listening. This is the richest and deepest support for individual discernment. Carmelite spiritual author William McNamara offers a simple yet profound definition of contemplation: a long, loving look at the real.[2] Contemplative listening, then, means bringing a full-bodied, loving presence to the person before you, as well as to what is said and what as yet remains unsaid. Contemplative listening seeks to honor the presence of the Holy Spirit in the speaker and between the listener and speaker. Such listening rests in warm, loving, engaged, and prayerful silence, which often needs few or no words.

Contemplative listening is more than simply not speaking. It involves putting oneself aside to attend fully to the other. When your own current or remembered experience begins to play in your mind, set it aside for the moment. I call this self-forgetfulness "bracketing" to convey the notion that one does not ultimately lose the self. Rather, one chooses, for this moment, to leave one's own concerns aside in order to be fully present to another. Any time your attention wanders from the speaker, it is time to bracket what you are then musing about and refocus your attention lovingly and prayerfully to the speaker. You can return to your own musing and memories later. This discipline also means that you must withhold your own pearls of wisdom, no matter how hard-won ("Let me tell you how I dealt with this same kind of thing—it worked really well"); your own similar stories ("The same thing happened to me"); and your own informed knowledge ("That's what I do in my job; I can help you"). Your best gift is your attentive, supportive presence.

Many groups choose to receive all personal sharing in contemplative silence—a silence that offers a very active and supportive response, as well as one that assures that the listeners will not subtly intervene in a member's discernment. On the other hand, other groups may desire to give some spoken response to each person's sharing. These groups add contemplative responding to their contemplative listening. In this case, some simple, yet difficult rules of speech apply.

In contemplative responding we act like a sounding box, taking in the speaker's words, letting them resonate within us, and giving them back magnified and made more resonant by our loving attention. We help the speaker, through our response, to hear more deeply what he or she just said. We do not move ahead of the speaker or begin nudging, however subtly, toward our own preferred interpretation or outcome. Short, succinct statements that summarize the speaker's words along with their underlying emotional tone are the most effective responses. Some typical starter phrases include:

"I heard you say . . . [repeat, in the same or similar words, what you heard]."

"It seems that you . . . [repeat what the speaker did or felt] because . . . [name the expression, action, or tone of voice that supports your educated guess]."

"I noticed that you . . . [describe something the person said or did, but without interpreting it]."

"There seems to be a pattern . . . [briefly describe the two or three aspects that link together]."

The briefer and more accurate your statement, the more helpful it usually is to the speaker's own contemplative process.

In the group setting, these simple speaking and responding rules protect the spiritual freedom of each person before God. If you want a more interactive response, for example, to talk over the various options appearing in your own prayer, simply approach one of the members (or your spouse or spiritual director) outside the discernment group setting, and ask to talk over your discernment.

Finally, rest assured that the most important activity in all that follows is simply to hunger for God's life to come more fully—in you, in others, in the world. All the rest is God's job. And God is faithful, beyond our ability to ask or imagine.

Our discernment begins, then, with the ancient Christian prayer beckoning the Holy Spirit:

Come, Holy Spirit, fill the hearts of your faithful.
Enkindle in us the fire of your love.
Send forth your spirit and we shall be created
And you shall renew the face of the earth.

PART ONE

An Invitation to Christian Discernment

1

Discernment: What Is It?

The term "discernment" seems to be cropping up in unlikely places—unlikely, that is, considering its roots as a Christian spiritual practice. In corporate boardrooms, management consultants teach discernment as a substitute for Robert's Rules of Order. Coworkers go on retreat to discern the new company advertising tagline. Hospital administrations discern the new mission statement for the health-care system. Young people discern their college choice and then their majors. "Discernment" often seems to be synonymous for decision making: instead of deciding, we now discern. But what is discernment anyhow? What are its roots? What theological presuppositions is it built upon? And how might we go about discerning? These questions occupy us in this chapter. We begin, as we will in every chapter, with a spiritual practice, a simple prayer of several steps. These prayer exercises are the experiential heart of this book; they are designed to move you from thinking about to actually practicing discernment. I invite you, then, to move out of

---

Practice: Awareness Examen

The Awareness Examen helps us look for the traces of God's actions in our daily life. It is usually done in the evening looking back over the day, but you may also use it to pray about any other meaningful period of time (such as a week or a year), or discrete event (such as a meeting or a class). Allow

---

between five and fifteen minutes for this spiritual exercise. This prayer is very flexible. You may use only the roman or italic lines, or you may use the entire prayer.

Give thanks for all God's gifts and benefits
Jesus, you have been present today throughout our world. . . .
I rejoice in . . .

Ask for light
Be near now. Let us look together at my day.
Let me see through your loving eyes. . . .

Review the day: thoughts, words, deeds, desires, consolations, desolations
When did I listen to your voice today? . . .
When did I resist listening to you today? . . .

Express gratitude, sorrow, and purpose of amendment
Jesus, everything is gift from you.
I give you thanks and praise for the gifts of today. . . .
I ask your healing in . . .
I ask your forgiveness and mercy for . . .

Ask for the graces you desire for tomorrow
Jesus, continue to be present with me in my life each day. . . .[1]

the activity of reading and into the disposition of prayer. Once you have completed the spiritual practice, you can become a reader again.

THE FIRST OF MANY PRACTICES

The spiritual practice called the Awareness Examen[2] is a contemporary renewal of the classic spiritual discipline called Examination of Conscience. "Conscience" describes that human capacity for distinguishing right from wrong, drawing us toward the right or better moral action. Examination of Conscience and discernment are related because they both rely on careful discrimination and choices about how to live our lives. Over time, unfortunately, Examination of Conscience came to be more and more restricted to naming sinful acts, and as that shift took place, it became easy to lose sight of God, focused as the spiritual practice became on human sinfulness. The Awareness Examen restores the focus on God; it literally shifts the figure and the ground in the practice. In the Awareness Examen, we look for and celebrate God's presence and action in our lives, and only in this context do we also notice how we might have fallen short in our response.

With this simple practice of the Awareness Examen, we begin to train our ability to notice, which undergirds our subsequent discernment. Over time, it helps us come to know ourselves in the light of God, and thereby come to know God. It helps us pay attention to our desires so we learn to recognize those that are life-giving. It hones our ability to notice what God is doing in the concrete circumstances of our lives. More importantly, it invites ever-deeper cooperation with God's desires for our lives. Retreat leader Timothy Gallagher says it well: "The prayer of examen is the specific searching *every day* to find where God's love is *active* this day, where God's love is *leading* today, to discern what within me may be resisting that leading and to discover the growth to which God is calling me tomorrow and that this deepest desire can be increasingly fulfilled."[3]

Ignatius of Loyola, the sixteenth-century founder of the Jesuits, was so convinced of the importance of the examen that he counseled Jesuits never to abandon it, no matter how urgent the ministry. He recognized that, practiced over time, it elicited self-knowledge, knowledge of God, humility, courage, and generosity for ministry.

Like our ancestors, we too might be tempted to slip into self-examination, forgetting that God is the point of this spiritual practice. Spiritual director George Murphy, SJ, suggests some simple advice to make this practice both personal and immediate and, at the same time, to avoid falling into unhelpful self-analysis. If his version helps you pray your awareness examination better than the version at the head of the chapter, by all means use it.

—Ask God to look at your day with you.
—What does God show you about your day?
—What was important to God from your day?
—Talk to God about your day.[4]

I strongly encourage you build the Awareness Examen into your daily life. The important thing is to begin an awareness practice and then keep at it because its fruits appear over time. Eventually, you will reap generous rewards not only for your practice of discernment, but for your growth in the life of the Spirit as a whole. Indeed it is not too strong to say that the Awareness Examen is itself a kind of intensive practice of discerning, not about a specific decision, but of God's presence in your day-to-day living.

DISCERNMENT IN REAL LIFE

Will discernment really make a difference in your daily life? Is it only for big moments, or will it matter in your day-to-day choices?

Kelley—not her real name—ponders the crossroad she and her husband face. She has long wanted to begin a PhD program, and now that her husband is settled in his profession, it seems to both of them that the time is right. But Kelley's biological clock is also ticking, and she wonders with increasing urgency if she should put off childbearing for the seven years that statistics suggest it will take her to finish her dissertation. And immediately following those years will come more equally grueling years of finding a position and teaching new courses while simultaneously publishing substantial and original scholarly works in order not to get bumped off the tenure track. How does motherhood fit into this picture? Or does it?

Tom, a widower with grown children, retired a few months ago from his job as an estimator for an international plumbing and steam-fitting business. He appreciates that he no longer feels as exhausted as in the past five years, and he certainly does not miss the drivenness of his former lifestyle. Yet he is beginning to find his days stretching before him with little to occupy his time and energy. He realizes that he must find something worthwhile to fill his time, but what?

Terrie and Jake have been dating seriously for almost a year. They are very much in love. Both in their early twenties, they expect to graduate from college in a year in Jake's case and two in Terrie's. Jake's major, history, does not lead directly into the job market, and Terrie's, human services, virtually guarantees long hours and low pay. They think, however, that they can live simply enough to make the economics work—at least until there are children. But looking at all the transitions they will face in the near future, they wonder if now is the time for marriage, or indeed if they are each personally mature enough for marriage.

Tim and Wendy have just returned from their church's annual mission trip, where they fell in love with a little Guatemalan orphan, Isabelita, age seven. Their own children, seventeen and twenty, will soon be on their own. They begin discussing adopting, trying to weigh their own desires against Isabelita's needs. Is it better to assist Isabelita from afar so that she remains in her own culture, or to bring her to the United States and raise her here?

Eighty-five-year-old Gladys ponders if now is the time to move out of the home where she raised her family: "I know I need more help, but a nursing home seems so final. Is this the right step? The right time? I don't want to fall someday and have the decision made for me."

Decision making is part of human existence. We have all heard such comments as "If I had chosen another school, I would never have met Jim," and "The decision to travel to Africa has had a huge impact. That trip opened up for me how empty my life is—and I never saw that before." Yet often our lives go on, day after day, and we scarcely attend to what brings greater life or dampens down the fullness that God calls us to. A young preschool teacher may not notice, for example, that she has become quite adept at encouraging self-discipline in a room full of four-year-olds. Or the busy executive may be completely unaware that the one drink before dinner has now become an alcohol-blurred evening. Through our decisions we quite literally become who we are.

We all face momentous decisions at key turning points in our lives. At those moments, we recognize that we are at a crossroad and ponder carefully which direction would be better for all concerned. In contrast, most decisions are about more mundane matters; we frequently make these less sweeping decisions without realizing that they are cumulatively shaping our lives. Yet, if we had to pay focused attention to every decision, we would sink exhausted into bed each evening. As discernment becomes a habitual part of your spiritual life, you will be able to process the small and large decisions with the attention and energy each one deserves.

The Christian tradition has long recognized the importance of decision making. Because our identity is formed in part through our decisions, the making of decisions is actually a privileged moment for growing in discipleship. Through our choices, we can become the person God is calling us to be.

Because our decisions are so central to our identity as persons and as Christians, we can look to the Christian tradition for help in the process of decision making. That help is called discernment. The Latin root of the verb "to discern" means to discriminate. Thus, in the Christian spiritual tradition, discernment refers to the process of sifting out what is of God, discriminating between that which expresses God's call and anything that runs counter to it.[5] Christians have been discerning from biblical times to the present, seeking to respond to God's call within their personal prayer and the worship of the faith community, their moral choices, or simply in the ebb and flow of ordinary life. Whenever we seek to answer such questions as "How is God present here?" or "How can I know what God is calling me to do?" or "Is this just me, or is this really God?" or "Is God calling us to go forward with our plan?" we are engaging in discernment.

Discernment, then, is the process of intentionally becoming aware of how God is present, active, and calling us as individuals and communities so that we can respond with increasingly greater faithfulness. Those moments in which we make decisions are privileged times in which discernment can make a big difference: in decision making, self-determination comes together with God's call.

Approaching decision making through spiritual discernment relies on awakening and honing the ability to recognize God's desires in each moment. It relies on actively seeking God's call in the very process of making these decisions. Furthermore, if consciously attended to in a faith context, discerned decision making itself can become a significant path for growing in the Christian life. Our practice of the Awareness Examen provides one of the best tutors for such awakening and sensitizing our hearts to the movement of God's Spirit as it moves in our daily lives.

WHAT ARE THEY SAYING ABOUT DISCERNMENT?

Because discernment deals with the mystery of God, it resists being confined to a single definition, escaping attempts to pin it down once and for all. Discernment has a long history in the Christian tradition, and it has not meant the same thing at every juncture and in every context. Each definition reveals as much about the perspective, context, and values of the one doing the defining as it does about the nature of discernment. If we examine and then combine a number of contemporary understandings, we can come to a better understanding of what it means for today.

1. *Discernment is a gift.* Paul lists discernment of spirits among the gifts of the Spirit in his first letter to the Corinthians (12:4–10). Discernment, then, arises from God's gracious initiative. We do not discern except that God works the work within us.

2. *Discernment is simultaneously a habit of faith.*[6] Although all is grace, there is also, in the mysterious economy of God's plan, a crucial role for human action. We choose to notice where God is at work, to believe in a larger plan than we can grasp in the moment, to hope in the goodness of the future promised by God, and to align ourselves with God's preferred future as it becomes clear to us. And we must do all this with sufficient consistency that it becomes habitual.

3. *Discernment is the desire to follow the Spirit of Jesus, who is present within daily life.*[7] For Christians, Jesus Christ is the author and finisher of our faith (Heb. 12:2). We have a model, Jesus, who lived and died at a particular point in history, and whose life as recorded in the Scriptures suggests the parameters within which we live. But Jesus is not limited to that time and place long ago; through the Holy Spirit, the risen Christ is still present with us today. We can rely, then, on the Holy Spirit to bring to mind that which we need to live out our Christian life today (John 14:26; 16:13).

4. *We grow in this gift of discernment through fidelity to a discerning lifestyle, which demands trust, includes failure, and matures through self-reflection and prayer.*[8] Nothing is wasted—neither success nor failure, happiness nor grief, faith nor doubt. All can contribute to our discernment because God is present in all.

5. *Discernment grounds the capacity to live a fully and truly human life.*[9] Through discernment we grow in the capacity to live in reality as God perceives it (the tradition calls the ability to see reality as God sees it "contemplation"), to act in ways that are as free as we can make them from inner and outer compulsions and that are closely attuned to God's purposes in the world. In discernment, we are constantly choosing life over death that we may live in the love of Yahweh our God (Deut. 30:15–20). In discernment, then, we move beyond avoiding evil. We seek, among good options, that which better aligns us with God's creative purpose.

6. *Christian discernment means living in such a way that the basic fact that we are daughters and sons of God shapes and colors our decisions, both small and great.*[10] We live differently because of discernment.

7. *Discernment is a process.* We gradually "put on the mind of Christ" (Phil. 2:5; 1 Cor. 2:14) every time we search out and choose that which

better aligns us with the Jesus of the Gospels, the Christ of faith. A discerning life, then, is composed of repeated discerning moments; likewise, each major discernment rests on many small moments of listening for God in the midst of everyday life. Our intention is that all our decisions will enhance this putting on the mind of Christ. To the degree that they do, we are fulfilling the purpose for which we have been created. In this fulfillment, we simultaneously experience our deepest spiritual freedom.

8. *Even though discernment is concrete, particular, and ultimately personal, Christian discernment is always set within the larger community of faith.* This community carries our faith when we are weak, preserves the long tradition of listening for God, provides a collective interpretation of the Scriptures, and calls us to actions that are good for us and the larger community of living things. Cut off from its communitarian roots, the power and veracity of Christian discernment can easily stray into viewing our own idiosyncratic interpretations—and even downright evil—as God's call.

9. *Discernment is a framework that enables us to join in partnership with God.*[11] It is not magic and does not yield complete certainty, but discernment provides us a privileged way to sort through the ambiguities embedded in our personal lives and in the signs of the times.

To summarize: Discernment means making a discriminating choice between two or more good options, seeking the best for this moment. These choices, while personal and conditional, are set within the community of faith and honor our previous well-made decisions. Discernment does not bring us absolute certainty, but rather operates in a climate of faith. Seeking to follow God's call moves us toward that which is better for us individually and for our world, and assures us that God will accompany us into the unknown.[12]

BIBLICAL FOUNDATIONS OF DISCERNMENT

Although we have already begun to locate the practice of discernment within Scripture, discernment rarely appears under that name in the Bible. Yet the practice, if not the name, undergirds the community's consistent search to ground its life within its growing understanding of God and godly living.

The Old Testament presents a long series of situations where individuals and whole communities had to make choices—not an unusual theme in ancient narratives. Think of Abraham, Isaac, Jacob, Moses, and the prophets, and of Sarah, Rachel, Leah, Tamar, Hannah, Ruth, and Esther, all of whom had to launch out onto unfamiliar paths at the request of a divine authority that does not always justify its demands.

Consider the prophets. They presented the community with the need for discernment. The community had to ask how it could know that this person, who claims to be a prophet, is in fact speaking the word of God. Gradually, the community gathered its wisdom on prophets and prophecy and decided as follows:

—Prophecy that made the prophet unpopular was more likely to reveal the word of God than a prophecy that made the prophet popular and well-liked; easy prophecies, those that were not controversial, while perhaps the word of God, were only verified as they came to pass.

—Any signs proposed by a true prophet must also come to pass.

—The prophet's advice or prophecy did not vary from the basic religion—though it could and usually did challenge some practice of it.

—The life of the prophet and the prophet's intentions had to be beyond reproach.

The fundamental justification offered by the prophets, was, in fact, their own experience of having come in contact with God. Clearly, these criteria are not completely objective, and the subjective element comes to the fore in judging the veracity of a prophet's experience of God. Hence, discernment was as much at work in the matter of assessing prophetic claims as it was in the decisions made by the individual patriarchs and matriarchs.[13]

Several Old Testament texts offer particular assistance for our understanding and practice of discernment. For example, in Moses' farewell speech we read: "Surely, this commandment that I am commanding you today is not too hard for you, nor is it too far away. . . . No, the word is very near to you; it is in your mouth and in your heart for you to observe. . . . Choose life so that you and your descendants may live" (Deut. 30:11, 14, 19). The Israelites were on the verge of entering the promised land, from which Moses had been barred. Moses assures the people that, even after he has died, God's word will still remain in the community. Actually, God's word is as close to them as they are to themselves; they have already spoken and internalized it; it is written within their hearts. The transcendence of God's word is here balanced with its immanence. God's word is beyond us, but it is also with us. And if it is with us, we are to hear it and do it. We have the beginnings, too, of a touchstone or baseline that will help us know if we are following God's call: God's word is found in life, not in death.

In the story of the prophet Samuel's call (1 Sam. 3:2–10), the discriminating judgment comes not to the boy Samuel, but to the priest Eli. We are told that the word of the Lord was rare in those days. Presumably, Samuel had no experience yet with which to discriminate. But Eli did, and after the third time that Samuel appeared before him ready to do his bidding, Eli realized that it was actually the Lord who was calling Samuel. So he taught Samuel the appropriate response of openness and generosity: "Here I am, for you called me. . . . Speak, LORD, for your servant is listening" (3:8–9). Interestingly, the word that the Lord spoke to Samuel is against Eli and his sons, yet Eli recognized its origin and accepted it as God's plan for his life.

We learn three important things from this passage:

1. One person may have the revelation and another grasp the meaning.
2. The appropriate response to any revelation is openness and generosity, and without that inner response, God's word may remain unarticulated or unrecognized.
3. When God's word becomes clear, the necessary response is to receive it, honor it, and act upon it.

In 1 Kings 19, we learn that God's Spirit, whom we will come to know as the Holy Spirit in the light of Jesus' revelation, can be found not only in the wind of creation (Gen. 1:2), or the fire and cloud of Sinai (Exod. 13:21), but also in the "sound of sheer silence" (1 Kings 19:12), at which Elijah came and stood at the entrance of his cave, awaiting the revelation of God. We learn that God will come as God chooses (John 3:8), God often speaks from within silence, and God's speech often stretches our categories.

In the New Testament, Jesus himself is the object of discernment, and serves as a norm for all subsequent discernment. Those who come into contact with him are faced with three questions for discernment: who Jesus is, what his life means, and how they will respond. Each Gospel explains differently who Jesus is. Lessons from each can be clearly identified. The discernment about who Jesus is and what his life means is especially pronounced in the Gospels of Mark and John, though they use different images and metaphors to frame their portraits of Jesus. Mark's Jesus is a powerful charismatic healer, and Mark is amazed at the disbelief that met Jesus' healing ministry (6:1–6). For Mark, knowing Jesus is more than knowing about his power; it is following on the way of his cross. In John, the major metaphor is belief: "These are written so that you may come to believe" (20:31). But because the revelation of Jesus unfolds slowly, sight, and therefore belief, in the Fourth Gospel is a process.

But not only do we have to discern who Jesus is, we also have to discern how our encounter with Jesus asks that we live. To help us, we look especially to Matthew and Luke. Jesus' Sermon on the Mount, for example, exposes values that mark those in Jesus' company: they are poor in spirit, meek, merciful, pure in heart; they mourn, hunger, and thirst for righteousness; and they are persecuted for righteousness' sake.

All the Synoptic Gospels, but particularly Luke, recall Jesus' teaching in parables. To understand the parables is itself an exercise in discernment.[14] For those who can understand their meaning, they offer kernels of truth and insight that point the way to God's preferred future: "Let anyone with ears to hear, listen!" peppers the text of both Matthew and Luke. But for those who simply see the parables as riddles—then and now—their meaning is opaque: "'Seeing they do not perceive, and hearing they do not listen, nor do they understand'" (Matt.13:13). Jesus has harsh words for this hardness of heart—it prevents the healing God has for them—but offers praise and blessing for the eyes that do see and ears that do hear. We too are invited to see and hear who Jesus is, and this very discernment becomes the channel for God's healing and empowering presence.

One of the Synoptic Gospels' more concrete helps for discernment is found in Matthew: "You will know them by their fruits" (7:20). At first glance, a choice may be full of ambiguity, but we can gain some clarity after the fact by examining the results. The fruits of one choice teach us wisdom for the next similar choice. Discernment grows by noticing and acting on just such accumulated learning, and sometimes after-the-fact fruit is all the evidence we are granted. Paul picks up this same theme in Galatians 5, where he offers a typical list of the "works of the flesh" (v. 19) and the corresponding "fruit of the Spirit" (v. 22). In the final chapter of this book, we examine the crucial role that fruit of the Spirit play in discernment.

Though the Gospels never treat discernment explicitly, as we meditate on Jesus' life and teachings, we internalize the horizon for all future discernment, and clarify the norm against which our discernments must be judged.

Chronologically earlier than much of the Gospel material, the Pauline letters offer helpful yet largely unsynthesized reflections on the Holy Spirit and discernment in general, though little on actual processes. It may be that these processes were sufficiently understood that Paul did not feel the need to comment on them or that Paul had been sufficiently involved with the churches to which he writes that he knew how they arrived at decisions. In any case, Paul understands that all believers have received the Holy Spirit (1 Cor. 12:13), and have been called to freedom (Gal. 5:13) and to enjoy the freedom of God's children (Gal. 5:1). This Holy Spirit enables Christians to interpret their Christian existence (1 Cor. 2:12) and to make choices consistent with it (Gal. 5:25). Each Christian is capable of and required to interpret his or her life before God in the concrete choices life demands.[15]

The Fourth Gospel and the First Letter of John provide the beginnings of a theology of the Holy Spirit upon which to base our understanding of discernment. The Last Discourse announces the existence and presence of the Holy Spirit. The Holy Spirit, we learn, is sent by Jesus as his emissary, and will bring to mind all that Jesus has said and done (John 14:26). The Holy Spirit serves as counselor, advocating on behalf of Jesus and enabling us likewise to testify to Jesus (John 15:26). The Holy Spirit is also the spirit of truth, abiding with us (John 14:17), speaking only what it is given to speak by Jesus and even declaring things that we could not have grasped had they come from Jesus' mouth during his limited time on earth (John 16:13). Taking our lead from this theology of the Holy Spirit, we root all discernment in the same Spirit, whose purpose is to animate the life of Jesus in us today.

Using this understanding of the Holy Spirit, the author of the First Letter of John sketches out a rudimentary theology of discernment: Different spirits exist, not all of which are holy; therefore all spirits must be tested. Jesus is the norm of that testing (1 John 4:1–2). The Holy Spirit is manifested in an inner experience by which we can recognize God (1 John 3:24). This inner recognition grounds our belief that God can be discovered through our prayerful sifting and weighing. An essential mark of being grounded in God through the Holy Spirit is confidence toward God (1 John 4:17); we can trust ourselves to this experience of the Holy Spirit, rightly discerned. Finally, the experience of the Holy Spirit completes and crowns other external revelations of God. When we test our own discernment, we will look for congruence with Scriptures, doctrines, and practices of the Church, as well as congruence with our own prior experiences of God.[16]

The Acts of the Apostles, especially chapter 15, shows us a community learning to act in discerning ways.[17] A controversy about the basic meaning of Christ for the new times has arisen, an issue beyond local variation and preference. The principals gather in front of the whole assembly, which has the responsibility to make the necessary judgment. The parties argue their positions with considerable passion; opposition is clearly part of the discernment process. We see one part of the church calling another to account, but we also see the community's submission to legitimate authority, and significant attention to building up and strengthening the fellowship in the implementation of the decision. Unity is a singular fruit of the Holy Spirit in this prototypical communal discernment process.[18]

The Christian practice of discernment has deep biblical roots, as this admittedly selective scriptural overview reveals. You will surely think of other passages as discernment becomes a part of your life.

THEOLOGICAL FOUNDATIONS

Throughout this discussion, certain understandings about God have been operating. Some conceptions of God, humans, and the God-human relationship facilitate the understanding of discernment; others make it more difficult. I want to make explicit my assumptions about God, humans, and the God-human relationship that are particularly relevant to discernment. It *does* matter how we think about God, how we imagine that God communicates with us, and how we determine our responses.

God is real. This assertion may seem self-evident, but, for many persons, it is a difficult assertion to live by. Christians of goodwill often fall victim to a kind of functional atheism in some parts of their lives, saying they believe in God, yet acting as if everything depended on human structures. Yet without a living, growing faith in the reality of God and the possibility of communication between God and humans, discernment makes no sense.

God is creator of all that is, not only of the cosmos with its immense scope, but also of each individual part of creation. Furthermore, God did not just create once and then leave creation to "do its thing," but God is involved continuously in upholding and enriching the ongoing creation. God is not dead but very much active, "laboring on our behalf," in the words of Ignatius of Loyola.[19]

God created human beings with deep intelligence; with an ability to reflect on ourselves, on God, and on other creatures; and with the ability to choose, to direct our own future, and to affect other creatures around us. In one of the final points in his *Spiritual Exercises*, Ignatius puts these three assertions about God this way:

> I will consider how God dwells in creatures; in the elements, giving them existence; in the plants, giving them life; in the animals, giving them sensation; in human beings, giving them intelligence; and finally, how in this way he dwells also in myself, giving me existence, life, sensation, and intelligence; and even further, making me his temple, since I am created as a likeness and image of his Divine Majesty.[20]

God's provident care took human form in Jesus, who becomes our premier source of understanding, both of who God is and also how we are to live to be in harmony with our Creator. Jesus, in his turn, sent us the Holy Spirit to be with us and teach us all that we need to know. Jesus concluded his work on earth by saving us through his self-emptying death. The work of our salvation is thereby completed, and is available to us through belief in Jesus and expressed in baptism. Jesus, then, is the ultimate norm of discernment.

Speaking about God leads to speaking about humans. As John Calvin reminded us, there is a necessary connection between God-knowledge and self-knowledge. The first statement in the Shorter Catechism of the Westminster Assembly is in response to the question, "What is the chief end of man?" We reply, "To glorify God and to enjoy him forever." Ignatius wrote, similarly, "Human beings are created to praise, reverence and serve God our Lord, and by means of this to save their souls."[21] Carrying out this end, with its varied expressions in our individual lives, will bring our greatest fulfillment. The goal of human beings connects with the goal of discernment as we ask, "Which choice aligns me most clearly with the end for which I am created? Which of these options brings the greatest praise, reverence, and service to God?"

But as soon as we speak about the end of humankind, we must recognize our deep propensity for rebellion, sin, confusion, and isolation. Paul stated our predicament powerfully: "For I do not do what I want, but I do the very thing I hate" (Rom. 7:15). This fallen condition does not just affect individuals, but everything touched by human hands.

Human sinfulness affects our discernment as well: we are always prone to self-deception and to choosing penultimate or hollow ends over our true end. In our discernment, then, we need checks and balances lest we unwittingly be led astray.

Several thorny issues surround what could be called God's plan, God's will, or, as I prefer, God's call. Is it even possible to know God's plan? Deuteronomy 30:14 tells us, "The word is very near to you; it is in your mouth and in your heart for you to observe." But are we to understand God's plan as transcending creation, as a blueprint for how everything fits together? In that case, our job is to figure out what that plan is so that we may conform to it. This theological orientation encourages combing the Scriptures for clues about how we are to behave in our everyday life. Or perhaps God has already figured out who will be saved and who will be lost. If so, discernment doesn't really make any difference; God's will grinds on inexorably. These theological issues have divided Christian communities. Without presuming to resolve them, there is a way to understand God-human communication that leaves room for discernment.

This understanding begins with the universe as a whole: it is open, flexible, and evolving. On our human level, we experience the bound-edness that we call the laws of nature. But when we look either more macroscopically or microscopically, we begin to see that the universe is dynamic and ever-changing. Think of the mind-boggling theories of the origin of the universe or the science of quantum mechanics. Since the universe reflects its maker, we can expect that God, too, is dynamic, ever-changing, continuously creating—not simply repeating what has already been created. And since we are created in the image of God, we are able to participate, with God, in the creation of our future. Of course, humans are not free to the degree that God is. We are limited from within by, for example, a particular genetic structure that predis-poses us in certain ways; the particular culture, political system, and family into which we have been born; and our gender, socioeconomic status, and ethnicity. We are also limited by our own choices: when we choose one thing, we cannot simultaneously have every other option. Yet alongside these limitations, there exists in us a genuine ability to co-create with God our particular futures, as well as to contribute to the collective future of our communities, and indeed, of everything living on earth. We exercise this co-creative potential through our choices, lim-ited though they may be.

Put another way, all humans face an uncertain future, and we must live into it by the decisions that we make. We are creatures whose deepest self-realization comes from moving into God's future with all the life and skill with which we have been endowed, within the concrete situations of our particular and finite lives. Our fulfillment, then, lies in becoming the deepest, most alive person that we can be and that our concrete situations will allow.

In God's provident care, we have means of grace that help us to live as daughters and sons of God and grow into persons who live intentionally and richly in the midst of our concrete situations and limits. These means of grace include:

—The Scriptures—the normative texts for Christian faith and life. Yet Scriptures are also ambiguous and need themselves to be discerned. We must remember that they resist a single interpretation or right answer, straining toward more complex realities. Discernment of Scripture proceeds through sound scholarship, inspired preaching, and the witness in the community of faith. Good Christians, however, can interpret Scripture with varying emphases and outcomes.

—Tradition—the witness and teachings beyond the Scriptures that have proven helpful for nourishing Christian life and faith. Again, the tradition must be discerned in order to be brought to bear with integrity in particular communities and individual lives.

—The community of faith—which retells the stories of faith and nourishes the life of believers, through Word and sacrament, witness, bearing one another's burdens, and deeds of justice and mercy. This community, either collectively or through trusted and wise individuals, is one of the chief supports for discernment.

—The sacraments—those ritual actions that witness, celebrate, and affect growth in the life of the spirit within the lives of believers.

—Rich forms of prayer and devotion that nourish individual lives of faith. Finding the best spiritual practices for each individual is often a matter for discernment. A life of personal and corporate prayer is the single most important preparation for discernment.

One more thing about God: it is impossible to fall outside God's love, no matter what we do or don't do. As the psalmist asks us, where can we go to flee from God's Spirit? Even in our mother's womb God is present (Ps. 139). Whether this reality comforts or frightens us will have much to do with our willingness to enter into discernment. It is no accident that Ignatius of Loyola set his processes for choosing a state in life squarely in the middle of lengthy contemplation on the person of Jesus as revealed in the Gospels. Coming to know this God personally and intimately through the life of Jesus of Nazareth gives us the strongest grounding for our discernment and helps us to believe that, no matter what the outcome of our discernment, God's Spirit is still with us.

These are some of my theological assumptions. It is well worth paying attention to yours as you begin to practice discernment. Whatever yours are, they will, as all theological assumptions do, color your reflections, set parameters for your imagination, and indicate the scope where you feel able to act. Being clear about them will help your discernment; conversely, discerning can uncover assumptions of which you may yet be unaware.

PULLING IT ALL TOGETHER:
SEVEN STEPS FOR DISCERNING A DECISION

How does one go about making a decision by means of discernment? I propose that discerned decision making proceeds in seven interwoven steps, which represent the components of a decision made by way of discernment. The steps represent a logical progression from the beginning to the end of a decision arrived at through discernment. Events in real life, however, can be less of a straight line and more of a circle; with discernment, you may expect to find that the progression of these steps is less linear than I suggest here. More importantly, some steps must be repeated regularly (1, 4, 6, 7), and some can change midstream (2, 3). Nonetheless, as you'll discover, these seven steps will always be part of your discernment:

1. *Seek spiritual freedom, the inner disposition upon which discernment rests and which creates the climate for discernment.* Indeed, without this basic intention of seeking spiritual freedom, discernment collapses into self-assessment, self-improvement, or decision-making techniques—all of which can be good and helpful, but they are not discernment. The foundational attitude for which we pray is that we might desire what gives God glory more deeply than we desire any other created reality. This spiritual freedom is so radical and so beyond our power to create in ourselves that it brings us face to face with our own poverty and our need for continual prayer. Sometimes all we can muster is the *desire to desire* what God desires! But any degree of hunger, any desire for God,

any seeking of God's call already happens through God's Spirit, and God accepts it as enough. Over time, through repeated discernments and through daily living of one's Christian life, this desire can become an increasingly natural and habitual orientation. As that transformation occurs, we experience deeper and deeper spiritual freedom.

2. *Discover and name the issue or choice you face.* What is really at stake is not always self-evident. An ambiguous or sprawling issue can obscure or even prevent subsequent discernment. Carefully framing the issue not only helps to clarify the matter for discernment, but it also actually begins the process of sifting and discriminating that is at the heart of discernment.

3. *Gather and evaluate appropriate data about the issue.* Discernment is not magic. We have to do our homework. The efficacy of the subsequent decision can rise or fall on obtaining accurate and relevant information about various options and their implications. However, since decision making is not identical to discernment, it is possible to botch a decision while still advancing in discernment. Fortunately, through grace, it is quite possible to grow in discipleship, manifest greater spiritual freedom, and hunger more strongly for what God desires in the midst of a failed decision. But prudence demands that we do the homework necessary.

4. *Reflect and pray.* Actually we have been praying from the outset. We pray for spiritual freedom. We select and frame the issue for discernment in prayer. We prayerfully select and consider the relevant data. But as we begin the process of discrimination in a more focused way, it is important to renew our attention to prayer.

5. *Formulate a tentative decision.* Many different methods can help us come to a decision, and therefore aid our discernment. We will explore seven methods in the entry points in this book, but many options exist in the tradition. Discerned decision making can employ any decision-making process, whether traditional or newly created, that fits the material being discerned and that allows us to proceed with the necessary disposition, seeking God's call. Notice, however, that the decision made at this point is only tentative. Another important step follows.

6. *Seek confirmation.* In this step, we bring the work we have done, including the decision that is emerging, back to prayer, asking God to confirm it. That is, we await the inner sense that we are on the right track. We look for the presence of indicators, the touchstones or norms that the tradition suggests are signs of the Holy Spirit's work. We bring our tentative decision to the community of faith, checking our sense

with others who know us well. In confirmation, we "discern the discernment." We "test the leadings."

7. *Assess the process.* Still discernment does not end. We look back over and examine the entire process. Was there anywhere that we acted without spiritual freedom? Any place where peace deserted us? Any part filled with anxiety? We let some time pass and look to see what kind of fruit has appeared in our lives and the lives of others as a result. This final look back can deepen both our conviction that we have chosen with deep integrity and that God will be with us as we live into the implications of our decision. But if something went awry, we can become alert to how that happened and therefore more attentive to preventing it in the future. Nothing need be lost.

All good decision making focuses the question, collects and assesses important and relevant data, uses a variety of processes to reach a decision, and looks back to evaluate the process. But the first, fourth, and sixth steps are unique to discernment in decision making. In discernment, we begin with the desire to follow God, we pray at every step of the way, and we bring our tentative decision back to prayer one more time for God to confirm it.

In effect, these seven steps outline the remainder of the book: Chapter 2 expands the notion of spiritual freedom as the foundation for all that follows; chapter 3 leads us through discovering and framing the issue for discernment and gathering appropriate data; chapters 4–10 enlarge on the fifth step, formulating a tentative decision, providing seven methods for prayerfully coming to a decision; and in chapter 11 we learn to seek confirmation and look back over the process.

FREQUENT QUESTIONS

People who are learning about discernment regularly ask several questions:

1. *When should we use discernment in our decision making?* Actually, I hope we will bring the attitude of desiring to seek God to all our decisions, and as our lives become more conformed to God's call, all our decisions, even small ones, flow from this conformity, almost without our conscious awareness. I encourage you to use discernment consciously and somewhat formally, however, when you know you are approaching a major decision.

2. *Does discernment cover the discrimination between right and wrong, good and evil?* When the choice facing us is between an ethically evil

action and a neutral or good one, discernment, strictly speaking, is not at issue. God could never be calling us to do something evil. We don't discern whether or not to cheat on our income tax, for example. In a world of moral ambiguities, however, the difference between good and evil may not be so very clear, and discernment may assist us in these ambiguous situations. We may very well discern whether to tithe our income, or whether we should withhold our income tax for matters of conscience. As a Christian spiritual discipline, discernment is appropriate when one is faced with deciding between two "good" choices, between a "good" and a "better" choice, or sometimes to help sort out morally ambiguous choices.

3. *How sure is discernment?* You might wonder, how can I ever be certain that I am doing God's will? Absolute certainty is impossible. We can never do away with the need for faith. What we do achieve is a relative certitude about our decisions, knowing that we have carefully and consciously tried to dispose ourselves to hear what God might be saying to us and to remove any obstacles that might prevent us either from hearing or from putting our decisions into action. This kind of moral certitude is all God asks of us, given our finite capabilities.

4. *Does discernment always lead to the right decision?* Answering this question depends on the meaning of "right." If by "right" we mean that decision which corresponds most closely to God's call, which flows out of our deepest, best selves, the answer is yes. If "right" means turning our powers to hearing and following as best we can, then surely the answer is yes. But a common error in discernment is to assume that, once we have discerned, the outcome of the decision should also be clear or that everything should work out as we imagine it. Not necessarily. Making this assumption leads to all kinds of confusion. For example, suppose a family carefully discerns that they should sell their house, pick up and move across the country in order to take advantage of a new work situation, only to arrive there and find the job market dried up. In this sense, discernment may not yield the "right" answer. In terms of the choices open to us, our decisions may be qualified by the data we have gathered—or not. We will also still be subject to forces we can't anticipate. God does not protect us from these. However, God does not abandon us in the midst of these unforeseen circumstances, and we may rightfully say to God, "Now what?" knowing that we have done our best to hear and respond. Discernment, then, is not getting certitude about the outcome or being right, but seeking God in and through our decisions.

And God wants to be found.

2

The Foundations of Discernment

Great desires, passions, motivations, loves and hates, and the decisions that flow from them—this is the stuff of discernment! Discernment is far more than the decisions we make. It is a discriminating way of life, in which we come to notice with increasing ease and accuracy how our inner and outer actions affect our identity in God. Practicing discernment in decision making is but one aspect of this whole way of life.

In this chapter, we probe five of the foundations of this discerning way of life: the importance of desire in discernment, the experience of understanding ourselves as simultaneously loved and saved sinners, our role as co-creators with God, the meaning and practice of spiritual indifference, and the call to desire more in our lives. You will learn three practices that will help you begin to internalize the foundations upon which your subsequent discernment rests.

DESIRES AND DISCERNMENT

Sigmund Freud once observed that dreams are the royal road to the unconscious. In discernment, desires are the royal road to self-knowledge. And, as John Calvin pointed out clearly, self-knowledge is directly linked to knowledge of God.[1] That is, when we know our deepest desires, we know something important not only about ourselves, but also about God, as our deepest desires come from and point to that same

Practice: Seeking Your Heart's Desire

Desires play a key role in discernment; they help us bring our whole selves to God. Here you will begin to identify your heart's most basic desires. Prepare yourself to pray by attending first to your body, to any tensions, fatigue, lightness, or energy that it carries. Then attend to your mind, with its busy humming and noisy chatter, its naming, judging, and planning. Invite your body to relaxed attentiveness and invite your mind to take a break for the next few minutes. Paying gentle attention to your own breathing, without trying to change it, may assist your efforts regarding both your body and your mind.

1. Dedicate this time to God. Ask for the light of the Holy Spirit to notice your deepest desires, to name them accurately, and to respond appropriately to what you find.

2. When you are ready, ask yourself, as you sit quietly in the presence of God,

"What do I want, right this minute?"

3. When you recognize what it is that you want, give it a name and jot it down in your journal. Return to the relaxed attentiveness. Ask again:

"What do I want, right this minute?"

4. Again, notice, name, and jot it in your journal.

(Repeat this process, until no more desires surface. After each, return to your relaxed attentiveness.)

5. Now look at all the desires you have named. Notice which seem to be the most central, the most important, the most attractive, the most full of energy. Select one that, for now, seems most central, and bring it back directly into your attention.

6. Without judging it (or yourself), ask,

"And what is underneath this desire? What desire is even more basic than this one?"

7. Gently repeat this question for each subsequent desire that surfaces. Ask each one,

"Is there an even more basic desire underneath this one?"

8. When you come to the deepest desire, honor it as central to who you are.

9. Finally, offer it back to God, just as it is, as an expression of who you are at this moment.

God. Desires are also powerful expressions of our passions, and these passions are what move us to action. Thus, when we know our desires, we will also be alerted to the potential for our most powerful actions—for good or ill. When we are attuned to our desires, we notice when they conflict, sending us into an inner struggle and draining energy from other, more important issues.

Desires, however, are ambiguous. They can be signs of and distractions from our true direction. They can be an authentic expression of who God has created us to be, or they can represent impulses that are not central to our God-given identity. Therefore, knowing and being able to evaluate our desires is essential in discernment. The spiritual practice at the outset of this chapter, "Seeking Your Heart's Desire," gives us a way to begin to notice what our desires actually are, without judging them. In the presence of God, we simply let them surface, and seek to identify progressively more significant desires. As we find them, we offer them to God as expressions of our very self.

Ignatius of Loyola provides the clearest guidance about the place of desires in discernment. He himself was clearly a person of strong desires, and perhaps it was watching how his own desires motivated and propelled him forward but also got him into major dilemmas that caused him to reflect on the role of desire. During the days of intense prayer that make up his *Spiritual Exercises*, he frequently directs the retreatant: "Ask for what you desire," and then suggests what that desire might be. In the Contemplation on the Incarnation, for example, he writes: "The Third Prelude will be to ask for what I desire. Here it will be to ask for an interior knowledge of our Lord, who became human for me, that I may love him more intensely and follow him more closely."[2] He seems to be saying, "Here is the most important thing to desire as you pray this exercise."

Ignatius did not believe, nor should we, that every desire is equally worthy of careful nurture. Which of my desires are worthy? How do I tell the difference? For Ignatius, noticing the shifting of desires becomes the stuff of discernment of spirits.

Before we can get that far, however, we have to believe that our individual desires are, in fact, significant enough to give them our attention. If we believe that what we desire doesn't matter, that someone else will tell us what is important, or that any desire that we have will likely be contrary to what God desires, we are unlikely to trust our desires—perhaps even to know what they are. Nor will we be able to know who *we* really are. Our identity is expressed in those things we commit to as revealed by what we most deeply desire. But our deepest loss will be that we are unable to discover the true core of our longing that could lead us more deeply into God—a core that is expressed through our desiring.[3]

As we seek our deepest desires, over time we will begin to notice several things. We notice, for example, that we are bundles of conflicting desires. Culture bombards us with thousands of messages daily about what we should want. I had no intention of wanting a new wide-screen TV, for example, but I walked by the display the other day (of course, all the sets were on), and it became easier to want a TV with that clarity and color. It does certainly beat my hand-me-down seventeen-year-old set. But do I need it? No, though now a part of me wants it. I was in the department store in the first place because my washing machine of uncertain age was past repairing. I intended to get the basic model that washes, rinses, and spins. But then I saw the super-energy-efficient front-loading machines. Less water and less energy. Good things? Of course. Then I wanted the better machine. Multiply these small dilemmas by the literally thousands of messages that the culture sends: You really need . . . You can be more eye-catching if . . . Your business can make more money if . . . What really matters is . . . What *does* really matter is not always clear. To recognize it, we have to know who we are and where we are going, matters for discernment.

We may not always recognize many of our desires, even long-held ones. As I go around and around a particular issue, my spiritual director is apt to break into my circular reasoning, saying, "Yes, but what do you really *want*?" Or, "What do *you* really want?" Once I am able to identify what I want, then we proceed to weigh all my conflicting wants, looking for my deepest desire. Against that deepest desire, I can then get some clarity about the relative significance of the options available to me.

Psychologists give the name "resistance" to a particularly troublesome version of not recognizing our desires. Resistance is the force exerted over what we consciously desire by something else that we, often unconsciously, desire more. The rub comes because we are not conscious of the very existence of this conflicting desire. Philip Sheldrake gives an excellent example of resistance while making a point about how desire gives energy and direction to the psyche:

> I discovered [the power of desire] for myself in a fairly straightforward way when I was finally able to give up smoking after some twenty-five years. I had known for a long time that it would be a sensible thing to do, and in that sense, I hoped for it. The problem was that on another level I still found that the enjoyment of smoking outweighed my sense of abusing my body, and therefore myself. And so every effort to give up broke down after days or weeks. This went on for several years until finally, during a period of sabbatical leave, I said, "I do not *want* to smoke. I positively *desire* to stop. I am going to stop. And somewhat to my amazement, I did stop.[4]

Until Sheldrake was able to recognize and change the more basic desire of wanting the enjoyment that smoking gave him, he was not able to mobilize the will to stop. Similar situations are played out over and over in each of our lives. We, like Paul, do that which we would not and do not do that which we would. Sometimes, we catch a glimpse of what we *really* desire that has been outside our awareness. When that happens, we can then ask for the grace to desire something closer to whom we want to become. But at times, the conflict may be too strong, or the desire too far from our conscious mind, or the price seemingly too dear to pay. Then all we can do is cast ourselves on God's mercy, and ask for the desire to desire differently. That small willingness is our part. With this bit of cooperation, just our desire to desire, God can begin to change our hearts.

As we gain familiarity with our desires over time, we become more aware of a serious internal problem: we are divided at root. Thomas Merton, no stranger to desire, recognized the dilemma in himself: "In order to become myself I must cease to be what I always thought I wanted to be, and in order to find myself I must go out of myself, and in order to live I have to die. . . . The reason for this is that I am born in selfishness and therefore my natural efforts to make myself more real and more myself, make me less real and less myself, because they revolve around a lie."[5] This self-estrangement is not in our power to fix. Though it has indeed been overcome, once and for all, we still live with its effects. Nothing can heal this inner division except to lean back into God's saving mercy, depending upon God to reveal our dividedness and help us choose to let our desires be purified, and then to act with greater integrity, however small our step forward.

As we do this, we will also begin to realize that our desires point us to our vocation, as Frederick Buechner observed: "The place where God calls you to is the place where your deep gladness and the world's deep hunger meet."[6] Buechner has qualified "desires" as "deep gladness" because not just any desire is worth a vocational commitment. Ignatius of Loyola recognized similarly that our deep desires need to be cultivated. He directs retreatants to learn about their desires by means of the examen, and then he instructs them to reflect on their vocational choice in light of the person of Christ. For Ignatius, there is no better context in which to bring our purified desires to the world's deep need than the presence of Christ.

Honest prayer allows us to structure our desires. As we continually bring our desires to God, flawed and partial and conflicted though they may be, we find that they begin to get sorted out.[7] Ann and Barry Ulanov agree: "Prayer enlarges our desire until it receives God's desire for us. In prayer we grow big enough to house God's desire for us, which is the Holy Spirit."[8] The daily Awareness Examen can become our ally in enlarging our hearts. Praying the examen through the lens of our desires helps us notice our conflicted desires, encourages us to hold them up to God's grace, and invites us to look forward and formulate desires to meet the next day's challenges.[9] Our prayer focuses our desire. Our desire inhabits our prayer.

Desire never stops affecting discernment. As we begin to locate and celebrate our authentic desires, we can then use them as a plumb line for our discernment by asking: does this action flow from my genuine desires?

Practice: Remembering Your Personal History

How have your decisions and actions affected the person you are today? This prayer exercise helps you write your personal history of sin and salvation. The purpose is to see yourself as God sees you, not to pass judgment on yourself. If you find yourself slipping into self-judgment, return to the first step and allow your focus to rest again on God's loving presence with you.

1. Let the silence deepen around you. Ask the God who has known you since you were in your mother's womb (Ps. 139) to allow you to become aware of God's loving presence that surrounds you like air.

2. In the presence of this loving God, review your life, simply and humbly noticing what has been. First, without judging yourself, allow the hurtful, isolating, negative, and sinful things you have done (as well as the positive things you avoided doing) to surface in your awareness. Note each of these memories in your journal, and, as you do, offer a simple prayer of sorrow.

3. Next, without judging or congratulating yourself, allow a parallel history to form, this time a history of significant blessings and graces you have received. As you note each of these memories in your journal, offer a simple prayer of gratitude.

4. Looking at these two lists, what would you now like to say to God? Say it in your own way, perhaps writing it in your journal.

5. Listen to God's words to you: "Though your sins are like scarlet, they shall be like snow" (Isa. 1:18). "The steadfast love of the LORD never ceases, [God's] mercies never come to an end; they are new every morning" (Lam. 3:22–23).

LOVED AND SAVED SINNERS

Another foundation for discernment grows out of our identity: we are sinners who are deeply loved and restored to our status as beloved sons and daughters. Prayerfully recalling our personal history helps us sharpen our awareness of this two-pronged reality. It is essential to grasp both sides of this equation deeply and experientially: we are sinners, *and* we are saved.

Unless we have a deep realization of our sinfulness, salvation becomes an empty word that has no relationship to our own life. We cannot personally realize what Jesus did, recognize how diligently the

Good Shepherd searches, or believe God's mercy extends to us. But the other part of the equation, to know that we are saved, is equally important. A deep preoccupation with the question "How can I know for certain that I am saved?" led Puritan theologians, including the renowned preacher Jonathan Edwards, to develop catalogs of signs to reassure the faithful that they were embraced by the loving arms of God and could relax into their salvation. Edwards's list of reliable and unreliable signs not only clarified this question for his parishioners, but it has also proven an insightful contribution to our understanding of discernment. (We will return to Edwards's signs in the concluding chapter.)

If we believe only one side of this equation—either side—we have no need for discernment. The sinner is lost no matter what she does, and the saved person has already "made it" and need not put out any effort. But holding together the reality that indeed we are sinners, but we are also loved and saved, gives us reason for discernment. We still express the ambiguity of our sinful condition, and we cannot know for sure what to choose. But we also know that our efforts to choose wisely are always honored by our loving Parent.

CO-CREATORS WITH GOD

As we noted in chapter 1, humans freely co-create with God. This assertion is crucial to the foundations upon which discernment rests. If you do not believe it, you will also not believe that you are radically free to choose, or that your choosing can represent God's call to you. Discernment will not matter.

First, a story. A young woman was talking to her retreat director about her rising sense of generosity and her willingness to do God's will. "I am just waiting," she said, "until Jesus tells me what he wants. When that happens, I will do it." Her director, pausing a moment, replied: "Did it ever occur to you that maybe God is waiting for you to decide what you want to do and will join you there?" The thought was totally new to her. As she and the director probed what it could mean, she began to see new possibilities and new responsibilities within the scope of her freedom. For her to choose was not, in itself, in opposition to following God's will. God's will could be manifest in her choice.

We, with God's help and guidance, are responsible to carve out our paths within the boundaries of our life situation.[10] Constructing a life is part and parcel of what it means to be an adult human person, and we may not abdicate this responsibility to another.

By itself, this responsibility could be an enormous burden. But again it is only half the reality. The other half is that it is God who created humankind with this ability to choose, and it is God who upholds our very act of choosing as an expression of God's own creative self-gift. God has endowed us individually with gifts of personality and the ability to make decisions. Since God has created us, God alone can sustain the deepest meaning of our lives. But God does not dictate every small matter, every detail of our lives. God leaves us quite free to determine the specifics of our lives, while at the same time providing us with a climate of love, care, salvation, and grace in which to grow to maturity. In fact, God's love becomes specifically incarnated in each free, unique individual.

In this context, we can understand God's will as dynamic, yet constant. It is full of ever-new meaning to be discovered as our life unfolds, yet it is also constant in its promise of grace, salvation, and ultimate care. We follow God's will through our ongoing relationship with God, who invites us to discover our purpose and meaning through our decisions and actions. Those choices reveal to us who we are as individuals, created, saved, graced, and missioned. By our human freedom we constantly uncover the will of God in an open, flexible universe.[11]

The phrase "God's will" can itself be subtly misleading, though it is deeply embedded in the Christian discernment tradition. It implies that God's will is a thing rather than a relationship, something "out there" that a person must discover and then do. Because of the open-ended and dynamic nature of God's relationship with us, I prefer to speak of God's *call* rather than God's will—for I believe that "call" is more reflective of the open, relational, and non-predetermined nature of God's relationship with us than the classical term "will" often connotes.

Making choices, we can now see, is one way we can participate in the divine life. Philosopher Beatrice Bruteau brings us to the last step, to our role as co-creators with God:

> Participation in the divine life means doing what the divine life does, and that is creating. Creating is an on-going activity, expanded from the present into the future, making things that are genuinely new. . . . If the goal of our life is union with God, the archetypal Living One, and if the improvisation of continuous radical novelty is the characteristic of the Living One, then when we are united with God, we find

our fulfillment by participating in this creative activity. And this fulfillment consists in continuing to create, world without end.[12]

As we discern, we are invited to answer the question: "In what way is God calling me to create through this decision which I face?" We can now understand discernment as the search for our future in God's preferred future.

Practice: Seeking Spiritual Freedom

The importance of desiring to follow God's call through your decision making cannot be overstated. The attitude of indifference—that is, being willing to choose what God desires over all the other lesser things we might also desire—is the essential starting point for discernment. As indifference takes root in us, it flowers into the spiritual freedom to respond freely to God's call. This prayer helps you form and deepen your indifference.

1. Ask for God's Holy Spirit to be with you as you seek to understand what God calls you to do and be.

2. Consider the following statements. Turn them over in your mind, and then allow them to take root in your heart. Speak personally to God about what they mean for your life. Spend enough time on each that it becomes something you believe and accept as your own.

   —You, God, have created all that is, and are even now creating me, just as I am.

   —You desire that I become my truest and most authentic self.

   —You put in me my deepest and most authentic desires, Creator God. I can know what you desire, God, as I ponder and understand these calls of my heart.

   —Yet some of my desires lead me away from my truest self, where you, O God, dwell. I do not always desire what you desire.

3. Using your own words, ask God to deepen in you the *desire* for what God desires.

4. Commit yourself, here and in all the subsequent prayer exercises that mark the successive steps of your discernment, to ask for the gift to desire what God desires, and as God's desire becomes clear, to choose it.

5. Give thanks to God for any new clarity and freedom that comes through this prayer.

SPIRITUAL FREEDOM THROUGH INDIFFERENCE

This prayer for indifference invites you to put God and God's call at the head of your agenda, to believe deeply that your best choice is that which is more pleasing to God. This intention is precisely what distinguishes discernment as a spiritual discipline from other kinds of decision making. What we intend through our discerning is to come close to God, to follow God's call, to respond to God's grace, to do God's will, to desire what God desires, knowing that in so doing we are choosing our greatest fulfillment. This intention, this desire, is more basic than any result of the decision itself. A concrete decision is only a byproduct of our more basic desire to follow God's call as we sense it through the decision before us.

Our first task in discernment, then, is to dispose ourselves to God's love, to become aware of God's presence, and then to frame our intention to follow God insofar as possible. This purity of intention is itself a gift of God. Our part is to sincerely *desire* it; God's part is to work it in us over time.

Ignatius of Loyola chose a word for this purity of intention—indifference—and used that word in a particular way. By it, he meant being as free as is humanly possible to follow the call of God. In order to be ready to follow that call, we must possess a clear eye and a balanced readiness. As he puts it, we must become "indifferent" to any other "created reality" than that which brings us closer to God.[13] Only God's call can have a hold on us; nothing else can determine our future. As good as that something may be in itself, only God's call receives this level of commitment. As we approach indifference, we winnow our values down to the most basic and essential one for a Christian: to praise, reverence, and serve God in all that we choose. We are, in fact, getting means (all other creatures) and end (following God's call) in their proper relationship.

It is important not to confuse with its spiritual meaning for discernment the familiar, everyday meaning of "indifference" as impartiality or lack of attachment. Were we to be so confused, we might feel that we should not care about God's creation, or worse, that we actively distance ourselves from it. Nothing can be further from the meaning of spiritual indifference. God's creatures are rich gifts to be enjoyed, fostered, and nourished. In fact, delving deeply into creation is one of the best ways to come face to face with the Creator. Who has not felt themselves uplifted gazing at a giant Redwood or huge ocean breakers in the aftermath of a storm? Who is not made more thoughtful by the celebration of a wedding? Who is more committed to life than those who have participated in birth? Whose mind is not more expanded by a thoughtful and well-constructed work of fiction? Ignatius of Loyola loved to go outside at night and gaze at the sky and the stars "which he did often and long," his autobiographical scribe Câmara relates, "because he thus felt within himself a very great impulse to serve our Lord."[14]

Ignatius instructs us to enjoy creatures as God's gift to us: "The other things on the face of the earth are created for the human beings, to help them in working toward the end for which they are created [to praise, reverence, and serve God]." But they are not to take the place of the Creator, something we are always tempted to do and frequently slip into almost unconsciously. Ignatius continues: "From this it follows that I should use these things to the extent that they help me toward my end, and rid myself of them to the extent that they hinder me. To do this, I must make myself indifferent to all created things,"[15] not preferring one thing over another, one condition over its opposite, one outcome over another. As it becomes clear how God is calling, then *that* is what I prefer.

"Indifference" has another common connotation: passionlessness. But this also is far from the reality in discernment. It takes passion to overcome addictions, compulsions, and inordinate desires of all kinds. In fact, true spiritual indifference channels passion toward that which ultimately satisfies more, benefits more, nourishes more, fulfills more, so that we move toward that option when it reveals itself. In fact, indifference impels us to do so. Reaching the point of indifference in discernment simply means no longer being bound to any single option, outcome, point of view, ideology, person, or strong impulse toward any single option. It means experiencing a freedom to choose what best nourishes both one's deepest happiness and the world's thriving.

Over time, the spiritual freedom that results from indifference becomes a fruit of discernment. As we make choices to join our lives to God's creative energy, our whole lives become a journey into greater freedom. One small freedom, responded to as faithfully as we are able at the moment, makes possible more generosity and greater freedom at the next moment. Little by little, day by day, we become more discerning and freer from compulsions, vices, addictions, and habits that pull us and those around us into greater chaos and fragmentation. One of the best aids to this growth is the Awareness Examen (chap. 1). The Awareness Examen provides a simple structure in which to look for the signs of God's presence and activity in and around us, and for how we join with God. The more we are aware, the more fine-tuned our responses can become. Discernment becomes a way of life, and spiritual freedom one of its lovely fruits.

You may wonder what this spiritual freedom will look like. How will you recognize it as it begins to appear in your life? Ecumenist Thomas Ryan points to four signs of its presence:

1. You develop a realistic sense of who you are. Self-acceptance allows you to be at ease with others and put others at ease with themselves.
2. You live your calling to the full. People who are spiritually free are tantalizingly alive, can take bold initiatives, are not paralyzed by the prospect of mistakes or failure, and can withstand criticism or even persecution.
3. You become free from any unhealthy attachments that come between us and the God who calls us, such as addictions, self-centeredness, or inordinate desires for power, wealth, or pleasure.
4. You daily rededicate your life to God.[16]

So, though at first blush, indifference may sound unattractive and out of place in the twenty-first century, when we look at it in relationship to the spiritual freedom that is its fruit, it can draw us very strongly! The virtue of indifference is one of the premier ways to grow in spiritual freedom; spiritual freedom is the goal of indifference.

Imagine what a community of spiritually free persons would look like. While acknowledging that such a community does not yet exist, philosopher Beatrice Bruteau has a picture in mind. In such a community, we'll live as beings called to radiate love and life to others. Sensual pleasures, emotional satisfactions, wealth and power, fame and influence—here she sounds very like Ignatius—will cease to be core values, so they will fade in significance. We will neither desire nor not desire them for ourselves and others. Finally, we will love others equally, but uniquely, so we will come to prize diversity as absolutely necessary for the thriving of this community.[17] Impossible? This "new creature" is precisely the reign of God for which we yearn.

GREATER DESIRES

If we are to contribute our best to the reign of God, we need something beyond our everyday vision and imagination. We need greater desires; we need "the more."

Ignatius knew that the most effective laborers for the reign of God would be those who could generate their own zeal. They would not have to depend on their environment providing all the right stimuli, or on feeling rewarded, or on receiving kudos from others; they would persevere through thick and thin to bring about the object of their desire. He developed a method for eliciting in his companions great desires that centered on cultivating the imagination and employing appropriate asceticism.[18] His strategy still works today.

If we can't imagine any other world than we presently inhabit, we will not desire more. To move toward deeper desires, then, we must school our imagination, learn to imagine that which is not yet. Scriptures, especially the prophetic books, urge us toward a vision beyond our mundane experience. Contemplative prayer clears out our old images and readies us for new ones given us by the Holy Spirit. Testimonies and the lives of strong and holy exemplars, of today's saints, can stir up our imaginations. We can associate with people who share our great desires or whom we admire, and let them stimulate our imaginations. When our energy flags, we can return through prayer and memory to our authentic desires, allowing them to come alive again.

The way to great desires is always pitted with conflicting desires, our own and those of others. We can remain divided in our desires, or we can engage in a struggle between opposing desires. A focused asceticism, or self-denial for the sake of greater purposefulness, can help us temper desires that dampen our imaginations and allow us to settle for less than God desires. Notice that asceticism is not for the sake of killing off parts of our selves, but for the sake of marshaling our full energy around our deep desires.

To summarize: desires underlie all our motivation; discernment urges us to choose well among these desires. Our experience as loved and saved sinners allows us to believe that discernment can happen. We can enter into a process of sifting through the ambiguities of our situation. Our experience as co-creators of God's unfolding purpose in creation underlies the importance of discerning well. It matters to the continual outworking of God's creative life. Growing in spiritual freedom through spiritual indifference is simultaneously the essential prerequisite and the goal of spiritual discernment. Without this spiritual freedom, discernment, as such, does not exist. With it, discernment becomes a powerful means of growing in holiness. Finally, seeking great desires, the "more," invites us to stretch beyond our limited horizons to do something great for God.

Ignatius's foundational statement about indifference, here rewritten to express it from God's point of view, cuts to the heart of the spiritual indifference that we seek before, through, and as a result of our discernment. It can serve as the foundation for each practice that follows:

_____ (Your name), the goal of your life is to live with me forever. I gave you life because I love you. Your response of love allows my life to flow into you without limit.

All the things in this world are my gifts, presented to you so that you can know me more easily and return your love to me more readily.

I want you to appreciate and use all my gifts insofar as they help you develop as a loving person. But if any of my gifts become the center of your life, they displace me and so hinder your growth toward your goal.

In everyday life, then, you must hold yourself in balance before all of my created gifts insofar as you have a choice and are not bound by some obligation. You should not fix your desire on health or sickness, wealth or poverty, success or failure, and long life or a short one. For everything has the potential of calling forth in you a deeper response to your life in me.

Your only desire and one choice should be this: to want and to choose what better leads to my deepening my life in you.[19]

PART TWO

The Practice of Discernment in Decision Making

3

Focusing the Matter for Discernment

You likely have a decision facing you right now. It's time to begin your discernment. Up to now, our discussion and exercises have focused on foundational attitudes and spiritual practices for the discerning life. You have also started to practice the first of the steps for discerning a decision laid out in chapter 1, seeking spiritual freedom through indifference. So significant is this foundational attitude that every exercise from this point on begins with this same desire for spiritual freedom, so that you can renew your intention every step of the way.

Now we move to the next two steps in discernment: (1) focusing the issue about which you will be discerning and (2) gathering data that impacts your decision. An exercise launches you into each step.

Practice: Framing Your Discernment Question

Clarifying the scope and content of your discernment can simplify the subsequent steps of your discernment process. This exercise sets that clarifying and winnowing of your issue or question within the context of a prayer that God will help you see clearly where you should focus your discernment.

1. Let the silence deepen around you. Enter into it. Ask God for the desire to follow God's call in and through the decision you will

---

be making. Do not rush. Simply turn your attention to God, as you experience God, and address your desire to God.

2. Describe the decision that you wish to discern.

3. Elaborate in your discernment journal the aspects of this decision that seem important to you at this point.

4. State as concisely as you can the decision before you. It will be helpful if you can formulate your issue in a question that can be answered yes/no (for example: "Should I begin to work outside our home?").

5. Bring the issue and the process you've engaged in thus far to God and attend to any thoughts or feelings that arise in you. Note these stirrings in your journal. Your first statement of the decision before you may shift; if so, repeat steps 4 and 5 until you sense that you have as clear and concise a statement as possible at this point.

STARTING WELL

Clarifying what is actually at stake in discernment is the first step in the process. Sometimes that process is relatively easy and straightforward, but frequently it's not. But unless we know what is at stake, we'll not know what information is relevant, how to prioritize the information we do have, or what options to consider, and we may have to backtrack several times and start again. Spending some time prayerfully considering what precisely your discernment will focus on will stand you in good stead later in the process.

Sometimes a complex issue can be broken into smaller, more focused questions. For example, Pete is a high-school junior beginning to think about going to college. As an issue for discernment, this decision is relatively easy to frame as a discernment question. He might state it: "Shall I apply for college?" If this discernment leads to "yes," the next question will probably be "What college?" This new question, however, raises some other issues: big or little institution? one that specializes or one that offers lots of alternatives? close to home or far away? private or public? The general question, "What college?" necessitates answering many sub-questions. This question, as broad as it is, needs to be narrowed. Pete can use each of the pairs of refinements as its own discernment question. For example, he might formulate the next question as: "Shall I live at home or away from home?" Proceeding through a series of smaller discernment questions, Pete could decide to attend a public university close to home. Discerning each focused question leads naturally to another, and with each repetition, his eventual decision is becoming clearer, the options narrower.

Of course, not all matters that we might wish to discern lend themselves to precisely formed discernment questions. With that in mind, some of the chapters ahead—particularly chapter 5, on using your intuition, and chapter 7, on using your imagination—may help you move toward a more focused question. Have patience as you work through this book, and remember that certain entry points into discernment will be more productive for you than others, depending both on your personality and the kind of question you are discerning.

Let me comment now on the various aspects of the prayer exercise with which you began this chapter. The prayerful framing of your discernment question begins by inviting you to pause and prayerfully ask for the grace that your spiritual freedom will continually deepen as you proceed in your discernment process. You are asking, in Ignatius of Loyola's language, to deepen your spiritual indifference. Remember, though, that God provides the resulting spiritual freedom; it is not something we achieve for ourselves. So we pause here, asking, expectant, knowing that desiring to join in God's purposes is the first step of any discernment. (If this step seems especially difficult—and it is not at all unusual that it would—return to the practice "Seeking Spiritual Freedom" in chapter 2. Repeat that exercise until you feel unstuck, flexible, and ready to move toward God's purposes for your life—at least a little!)

Steps 2 and 3 help you walk around inside the issue you wish to discern, becoming familiar with its contours, the feelings it stimulates in you, the desires it evokes, the relationships and structures it affects. You may discover other means by which you can become more familiar with your issue—for example, talking your situation over with someone who is familiar with it. Feel free to add them to the exercise.

As you describe the issue or ask the question in step 4, make your sentence as concrete as possible. It is much more difficult to get started if the issue you frame is vague, broad, or totally open-ended. For example, "Shall I study Spanish in Guatemala?" is much easier to tackle than

"Where shall I study Spanish?" But if you miss the mark a little and your question is too broad, don't worry; you can shift the question as you achieve more clarity. Even if the clearest you can get at this point is something like "What shall I do next year?" you can still proceed, though you may want to circle back later and repeat parts of the process as your discernment question becomes more refined.

As you finish this exercise, bring your issue and your process to God and write down what happens. You might note where you felt excited or de-energized, or puzzled, or stuck, for example. You might notice that you feel like you've named the issue correctly, or perhaps you have a sense that, while your question is in the general vicinity of what you seek, it does not hit the mark exactly. These observations will become important fodder for your ongoing discernment process.

Notice that the decision is the *occasion* for seeking God, not the primary goal. Setting out with the goal of making a decision that we then ask God to bless is to confuse the goal and the means. Rather, discernment involves the goal of seeking God through the means of decision making.

ASSUMPTIONS MATTER

Perhaps the greatest challenge in framing a discernment question is rooted in the fact that we all have hidden assumptions, things we take for granted without being aware of them, but which, if we can identify them, will greatly help us in our discernment. Suppose Pete, in the earlier example, had started with the assumption that he was headed for college and so framed his question as "Should I apply to City University?" As he tried to come to a decision on that question, he might uncover deeper questions glossed over by his original assumption and which he must grapple with before he can address his question: "Should I apply to *any* college right now?" "Should I take a year off?" "Should I go into the service?"

The assumptions we make as we begin discernment matter. If we simply assume that certain outcomes are untenable, undesirable, or impossible, we will rule them out of bounds before we even begin our discernment. But when we are aware of this self-screening tendency, we can instead consciously assent to those assumptions that match our values and consciously discard those that don't. The problem lies when our assumptions are not conscious; then we are unable to choose either to continue to hold these assumptions or to consider options that flow from them.

We can do three things to help identify our unconscious assumptions. First, we can make a habit of paying attention to what surprises us, or makes us anxious or defensive: Where do we not want to listen? Where do we insist on the opposite point of view? When is our reaction out of proportion?

Second, we can pay attention to those persistent behaviors that we seem unable to change even though we want to. We might say we want one thing, but find ourselves doing the opposite—quite like the apostle Paul's wry comment about his own life. The Awareness Examen (chap. 1) is particularly useful in helping us prayerfully notice and give over to God certain behaviors or assumptions.

Third, we can seek our deep, God-implanted desires. The spiritual practice Seeking Your Heart's Desire (chap. 2) can help you uncover your secondary desires, which may conflict with your deepest desires. Take Tina, for example. She wants to be honest in all her dealings. But when her supervisor asked her to overlook a little irregularity in bookkeeping, she found herself doing what she was asked. Puzzled, she wondered why she so easily gave up a value so central to her identity. Further pondering revealed an unconscious assumption had been operating: "I have to do what my boss tells me." That unconscious assumption overrode her deeper desire: "I am an honest person, and I want all my actions to proceed from my integrity." Now that she is clear about a previously unconscious assumption, she can take her fear about holding her job into consideration as she discerns an appropriate response that flows from her integrity.

Our assumptions are often culturally based. When I was growing up, for example, at around age thirteen, bright female students began to fall behind their male counterparts in mathematics and science. Although they were frequently unconscious of it, the assumption that "girls do not excel at these subjects if they want the boys to notice them" was lodged deep within many young women. Once that assumption was in place, it controlled the options that young women saw as realistic or desirable. Fortunately, this situation has changed to a great extent in recent years, but when I graduated from high school the majority of my classmates became nurses, teachers, or social workers or dropped out of college to get married. Few became doctors, lawyers, business executives, or scientists, married or otherwise. Our unconscious assumptions, reinforced by culture, college admissions counselors, the courses offered in school, and our friends and families, effectively limited the options available to us, in part because they became part of every decision we made.

Unmasking our hidden assumptions can be a lifelong matter. Becoming a discerning person is, too! We arrive at greater integration and wisdom by taking one step at a time, being willing to be as aware as the moment allows, as disposed to God as God's present grace makes possible, to ask continually for God's presence and guidance, and, when guidance does come, to learn to recognize it, and to follow it as generously as we can at that moment. Discernment, we see, is only superficially about making a single decision, even a momentous one. It is a continuous developmental process of becoming the more whole person God desires us to be. Our discernments *should* change as we change. Hopefully our spiritual senses become more acute as we learn to see God's creative presence in more and more areas of our lives.

GATHERING AND INTERPRETING INFORMATION

Practice: Gathering Relevant Data

The quality of a decision is directly influenced by the quality of the data gathered. That faulty data leads to less effective decisions is a truism whether or not the decision is made within a context of discernment. Just because we are discerning, we can't presume that God will magically make up for not doing this essential step. But what sets discernment apart from other decision making is that we do assume that the very process of data gathering can be set within the context of prayer—and that is the goal of this practice.

1. Pause as you begin this reflection and each time you work on the task of gathering data. Ask for God's gracious presence and help to seek out what is relevant to your discernment.

2. Ponder various kinds of information that will bear on your decision:

—Information about yourself, your personality, history, life experience, spirituality.

—Information about your relationships with family, friends, coworkers, neighbors, and enemies that will affect or be affected by the decision you are contemplating.

—Information about the groups, agencies, and entities that you belong to or interact with or that will be operative in the decision you are contemplating.

—Information about the human-made and natural environment, that is, the wide external context in which the decision is set.

—Other information that will help you make an informed decision in this particular case; including, for example, background leading up to the situation you are now discerning, knowledge of the players and their relationships, projected possible outcomes—that is, anything that could impact the decision or its outcome.

3. Imagine how you can gather this relevant information. Make a plan about what information you need to gather, and outline the information-gathering process in your journal.

4. Begin gathering necessary information. As you do so, keep a record of what you find out, assembling the relevant information in a form and in an appropriate place where it will be accessible to your continuing discernment. (This process of data gathering may continue throughout your discernment.)

5. Offer this reflection and the sometimes tedious homework of data gathering back to God. Record in your discernment journal how the growing amount of data affects your discernment. Speak to God about what it reveals: about the situation, about you, and about your relationships, especially with God.

"JUST THE FACTS, MA'AM"

When I was young, the television show *Dragnet* was very popular. Its lead character, Sergeant Joe Friday, had a catchphrase that has become a staple of popular culture: "Just the facts, ma'am." Sergeant Friday's phrase can help us at this point in our unfolding discernment process. We need appropriate and accurate information to make helpful decisions.

In discernment, we are, after all, focusing on our decisions and using them as a context for searching out and collaborating with God's call. Hopefully, we will make good decisions through discernment, and appropriate data is an essential building block to get there.

The facts we are looking for depend on the scope and focus of our discernment. If we are trying to discern the most fruitful way to pray, the data will come from things like observing our inner responses to various forms of prayer; from the fruits, inner and outer, that flow from various types of prayer; from our sense of being drawn to or repelled by various forms of prayer; from recognizing where we pray the most easily; and so on. If, on the other hand, we are trying to discern a job change, we need a very different kind of data: What preparation is required for the new position? Do I have it, or will I have to get it? How viable is it to think I will be able to land this kind of position at this time and in this location? Do I have any personal knowledge of the qualities needed or the climate in which I might be working? Does this kind of work draw on my personality strengths? How will this change affect my life and that of others around me in terms of time, resources, and financial remuneration? What are the specific conditions of the position I am considering? Can I work with the supervisor and the colleagues? What quality of communication and relationship exists among the colleagues? What data do I have that I would thrive in this type of endeavor? Are there ethical considerations, and can I live out my principles in this setting?

I cannot tell you in advance the kind of data you will need to search out or how you will interpret it. You will have to determine what is important to know as you head into a given discernment. It is often helpful to make a specific plan to gather the data, setting aside time and resources to do it. Such a plan is essential in the case of a life-changing decision, and very wise in other significant decisions.

Even though every discernment is unique, your search for data should always involve collecting four kinds of information:

1. Intrapersonal information (from within your unique self). Ask yourself: What are my personality and work preferences? Time, energy, and health? Economic resources? Do I notice that I am having any particular physical responses as I think about the situation? What do I deeply desire?
2. Interpersonal information (through face-to-face relationships). Ask yourself: Who are the people close to me who will be affected

by my choice? How will this proposed option be likely to affect my interpersonal relationships, especially with those close to me or with whom I have prior commitments, especially my family? What supporting relationships exist for me personally?

3. Structural information (from pondering those organizations, personal and impersonal, that exist regardless of the individual players). Ask yourself: What structures are in play here? What are their goals, their reasons for existing? What are their dynamics? What would be my role and responsibility in these systems if I were to make the decision I am pondering? How is power exercised? Who or what is marginalized in these structures, and what would they say if they could talk with me?

4. Information from the natural world (from the environment in which we are embedded). Ask yourself: What is the environment—the physical context, both human and natural—like? How does the human-made environment exist within or against the natural world? Is this an environment that invites or repels me? What kind of impact will my actions have on the environment?

After you've gathered your data, the next step is to interpret it, and it's helpful to use the same four categories as interpretive lenses:

1. Intrapersonal (your inner response). Ask yourself: Does the data give me energy? excitement? courage? confidence? tranquillity? satisfaction? Or are my reactions to it more like discouragement, anxiety, insecurity, agitation, dissatisfaction? Or, as is often the case, is my response a mixture of the two?

2. Interpersonal (the reactions between you and those persons close to you or who would be affected by your decision). Ask yourself: How do I feel about the possible effects of my proposed decision on those close to me? What do these people say about my proposed option? How do others who are more objective about the choice facing me interpret the information that I have received; do expert interpreters agree or disagree regarding the information I have uncovered?

3. Structural (what an analysis of the institutions, systems, and structures in which you live and work—or into which you would be moving—suggests about the matter at hand). Ask yourself: How will the various systems in my life have to be readjusted if I move in this direction: family, work, school, community involvement,

relationship to worshiping community, and so on? What values
are these systems preserving, and are these values worth it to me?
In what way are the systems likely to resist my proposed change?
What price could I pay? How does this feel to me?

4. Natural world (from the largest perspective, that of the grand
scheme of things). Ask yourself: Does being in nature tell me anything about my proposed decision? Will it, or how will it, affect
the environment? If I could stand on top of the world and look
down, how would this decision appear?

Let me give a somewhat extended example of these various kinds of
information and their interpretation from a personal discernment. I
once interviewed for a teaching position that I had long assumed would
be an ideal one for me. I would be returning to my hometown, which
I love, and I would be close to my family and religious community
(environment), who would appreciate my being close as much as I
would (interpersonal and intrapersonal). I would even be able to walk
to work, good for both the environment and my health. The salary,
while not great, was tolerable; the small increase, however, would be
offset by the somewhat higher cost of living in that part of the country (structural). The ministry department offering the position had
been recently reorganized in a way I thought I could work well in
(structural), but it was still completely separated from the theology
department, with different dean, curriculum, and students (structural),
which seemed odd and artificial to me. This separate but equal arrange-
ment had a long history (structural), and senior members of the faculty of the theology department argued for maintaining the division
(structural and interpersonal). The job description seemed one I could
enjoy, at least under certain conditions, and finding out whether these
conditions existed (structural) became one of my personal goals for the
on-site interview (intrapersonal). The persons who would be my faculty colleagues seemed personable, engaging, and welcoming (interpersonal), the students a little puzzled by my class presentation (personal
or structural, depending on the cause of this reaction, which I could
not determine during the course of my campus visit). As the interview
proceeded, I could not help but notice two striking things: as I was
asked about doing different aspects of the job, my stomach would
tighten into a knot (intrapersonal), and as I asked about doing things
I loved, I was met with the response, "Oh, that's not part of this job"
(structural), and the knot would return again. Needless to say, I came

home from the on-site interview clear that, if the position were offered to me, I would decline. The signs did not add up to a sense that God was calling me to move there. When the phone call came from the head of the search committee, I was not surprised that I was not offered the position. But I *was* surprised that the chair also admitted that they were not hiring any of their top candidates. During the course of the interview, they realized that they were really seeking a different kind of candidate than their advertisement attracted! They, too, had been discerning the responses and questions of their candidates.

As you can see, the process of data gathering and interpretation is far from incidental to the discernment process. Indeed, it is itself a significant step along the way.

A CRUCIAL DISTINCTION

Discernment and decision making are separable realities, as we have seen. It is worth noting this distinction again as we consider what kind of data will facilitate discernment conducted in the midst of major decisions.

"Just the facts, ma'am," as Joe Friday was wont to say, reflects the common wisdom about decision making: get all the relevant facts, line them up, evaluate them, and make the decision to which they point. In discernment we also want facts, and we also want to line them up and examine them and their implications. But because our goal is discernment in the context of decision making, there are two significant differences: first, we gather broader kinds of data and, second, we weigh that data differently.

That first difference was probably evident as you read the list of categories about which we gathered information and the lenses through which we evaluated that data. The scope of relevant facts is much broader, ranging from the very personal to the global. The breadth of the data you gather may surprise you, but remember that discernment data includes everything to do with our relationship with God, including our ongoing habits of prayer, the accumulation of insights from the Awareness Examen, and the results of the discernment exercises in which we will engage.

The second difference—how we weigh the data—shows up when we begin to interpret the data we have gathered. We are looking for signs pointing to the presence of the ineffable, the mysterious, and what we cannot completely know: the mystery of God's call to each of us as unique persons. We are looking for signs of the Holy Spirit, promised us by Jesus before his death. We are looking for clues given to us by the Scriptures, the Word of God to humankind, but we need the guidance of the Holy Spirit to interpret Scriptures and to see how they bear upon our concrete situations and decisions in this time and place. We need to learn to read this kind of sign, which is a very different project than lining up all the facts and making a decision based on them. Indeed, discernment is the art of interpreting all these signs, an art that we develop through our prayerful practice.

FRAMING THE QUESTION
AND SELECTING THE PROCESSES

The next seven chapters contain numerous exercises to help you with your discernment. You will likely find some exercises more useful than others. Your preferences may depend on the kind of issue you are discerning, how complex and significant it is and how precisely you can frame it. They may also depend on your personality, particularly how you prefer to make decisions.

Let's follow two people to see how they might profitably engage the practices in subsequent chapters. These two persons represent different scenarios for discernment and different kinds of discernment questions, and they rely more heavily on different processes contained in the following chapters. The first is an example from my own life. Several years ago, my religious congregation was preparing to appoint a sister to accompany the newest members through their time as novices. The selection process entailed gathering potential appointees and the person who would make the appointment, and together this group would discern who would be appointed. I have a heart for this work and had already undertaken some useful preparation for it, and with the encouragement of others who knew me well, I began to consider if I should participate in this group discernment—rather like deciding to apply for a job. Not yet sure that the position was a call from God, I began my own discernment to clarify if it were a call, and if I were asked, could I accept this call at this time. My question was, "Should I leave my name in consideration for the position of Director of Novices?" The parameters of this discernment were relatively clear—though it was not clear for some time how I should respond. The exercises for approaching discernment through imagination, rational processes, and religious affections (chaps. 7, 8, and 9) were especially helpful because they fit the kind of question and my personal preferences in decision making. Through them, I gradually came to the clarity and freedom that, if I were ultimately called to this position, I could do it. The clarity was sufficient to continue further into the community's group discernment.

Let's look now at a very different situation: Mary, a young woman two years out of college, is becoming established in her first professional position. Everything is moving along according to plan, except that she has noticed lately that she is restless. She does not know the meaning of her restlessness, nor as yet how she ought to respond. Should she ignore it? Start looking for another job? Try to widen her circle of single friends? Start dating a bit more? Mary's discernment question, very different from mine, is: "How should I respond to my restlessness?"

Mary's first task is to let her restlessness speak to her more clearly. Her practice of the Awareness Examen becomes more intentional, and she writes her observations in her journal. She notices soon enough that her restlessness doesn't abate in the wake of great weekends with her friends. When, during her annual job performance review, her supervisor has strong praise for her work and especially for her creativity, she realizes that she really doesn't care much and that her job doesn't feel particularly challenging and creative to her. This realization leads her to identify and pay attention to her desires, using exercises like Seeking Your Heart's Desire (chap. 2). On a long, contemplative hike, she feels the first notable spikes of energy in some time. She begins an intentional pattern: prayer and exercise in the morning to complement the Awareness Examen at the close of the day. She watches carefully for places, events, and persons that make her excitement rise. She begins paying attention to her dreams. She chooses the exercises that approach discernment through intuition, body, imagination, and nature, chapters 5, 6, 7, and 10, the processes that make room for "that which we do not yet see" to make an appearance and that build on her own preferences.

As she is praying the Intuition exercise one day, about three months into her pondering, an image, rich with symbolism, unfolds in her mind. In it she is leading a parade of little children, each of whom is holding the hand of the one in front. They are every color and shape, chattering excitedly. They are crossing the street under Mary's watchful eye. As she is processing this image, wondering what it might reveal, Mary thinks of the kindergarten children in the school near where she lives. She wonders, "Is my future with children like these?" She can frame her next discernment question with more focus: "Should I volunteer with young children?" To discern the possibility identified in this question, she employs rational processes and religious affections (chaps. 8 and 9) to help her clarify how she thinks and feels about it. Since her body registers energy or the lack of it, she also uses the body entry point (chap. 6). She wisely assumes that, even if the outcome to her discernment is "no, not this," it will still help her take another step in her larger vocational determination.

These two scenarios represent different situations for discernment and introduce different ways to use the exercises in this book. Your own experience and preferences will be different as well. Find your own way. Use the exercises that appeal most to you, of course, but also add at least one that you find less inviting to double-check the information you get from those you prefer. Seek counsel from friends, family, pastor, or spiritual director, especially when your issue is large or as unformed and vague as Mary's. But just because your matter for discernment is unformed and vague when you begin, it is not therefore a less-good discernment. God is still at work in your life, desiring to unfold rich choices in the midst of your very real situation. In the end, finding God is still the essential end of all discernment.

4

Memory's Guidance

We move now, in chapters 4–10, to the heart of discernment: making the critical judgment about what God is calling you to through the concrete circumstance of the decision before you. You have by now carefully framed your discernment issue and gathered the data necessary for a sound decision, all the while praying for the spiritual freedom to seek God through this decision. Now you will begin the process of making a tentative decision, gathering and assessing clues that will point you toward your decision. To do this, we will use a variety of entry points into discernment, each of which will suggest how God might be calling you through this particular decision. Each chapter contains several exercises to help you prayerfully notice and evaluate the subjective process that, cumulatively, points toward how God is calling you.

The way to the future sometimes comes to us from the past. Our first entry point into discernment is memory. Not surprisingly, here we use memory to surface clues about how God might be calling you through your present decision. We explore memory's ability to bring the past into the present, follow two discernment stories that make significant use of memory, and look at how Scripture models the use of memory in shaping our understanding of God's continuing presence. The first exercise, Approaching Discernment through Memory, outlines a way to pray using your memories. The second exercise encourages you to remember and reexperience the spiritual freedom that God gave you at some point in the past. Revisiting such a moment of freedom will give you a comparison point to use in evaluating the memories you surfaced in the chapter's first exercise.

Practice: Approaching Discernment through Memory

Our memories preserve, along with many other things, a personalized record of moments in which God has blessed, supported and guided us throughout our lives. This prayer opens us to recall one or more moments of God's support and guidance related to our present decision. The connection between then and now may be subtle and require some pondering, so take your time, especially when you get to steps 5 and 6.

1. Prepare yourself to listen to the wisdom brought to you through your memory by becoming still—outside and inside. Gently noticing your breathing may help you come to a deep quiet. Take as much time as necessary to come to this place of quiet.

2. Offer this time of remembering to God. Ask God to speak to you through your memories, and tell God of your desire to be available to God through them.

3. As you think of the decision facing you, allow your memory to surface a particularly graced event or period in your life. The memory may but need not directly resemble the issue you face at this moment. Relive that event or period and remember it in all its textures.

4. Notice how God was "laboring" on your behalf during that time. Notice, too, how you responded. Remember the grace of the moment. Capture in your journal the highlights of the grace and your response.

5. Notice the similarities and contrasts between your experience then and your issue now. Record the salient points in your journal.

6. As you relive that graced moment in your past, examine what it suggests about the decision before you now, thanking God for God's constancy.

MEMORIES: PAST IN THE PRESENT

Our memories give us the extraordinary power to re-create the past in the present. They can be potent tools for moving our discernment forward, but which memories from among the vast storehouse serve this purpose? The exercise above, Approaching Discernment through Memory, places our remembering in the context of prayer in which we ask God to bring to mind those memories that offer guidance for the future. Our memories can be close to the surface of our minds or buried more deeply and thus harder to access. Stilling our mental chattering can create a hospitable space for some of these deeper memories to surface. You may also notice that one memory can call up others, almost like a magnet attracts iron filings. In the context of this prayer, one memory of God's grace may lead to others.

We tend to take memory for granted until we or someone we love cannot remember any longer. Losing one's memory is a tragedy, not only for those to whom it happens, but for those in relationship with them. Without memory to connect the fragments of one's life into a continuous narrative, the personality begins to unravel and become disconnected from reality. When my mother was recovering from a small stroke, she went through an episode of memory loss. I brought pictures to the hospital and showed her all the people in the family. She looked at a picture of me as a child and said, "Who is that?" "It's me, Mom," I replied, "your daughter." She looked at me blankly. The next day, when I went in, I asked her if she knew who I was. "Yes," she said promptly and proudly, "you're the woman who brought me flowers yesterday."

Without her memory, my mother's past neither hung together into a continuous narrative nor connected to the present. She was no longer able to "be" my mother. I was the woman who brought her flowers and who showed her pictures that had no relation to her life. Fortunately, a few days later, when repeating the picture exercise, she recognized my sister-in-law, and within a day or two, the threads of her memories began to reweave the narrative of her life and connect the relationships of the past to the present. She was my mother, and I was once again her daughter.

We can return to a memory over and over. Memories appear to be fixed and stable, or so we think. But memories are also idiosyncratic and flexible. Three persons witnessing the same event and recalling it later will reconstruct the event differently. When family members share reminiscences, someone sooner or later says, "Do I ever remember *that* differently!" or "You've got a lousy memory! It really happened like this. . . ." Memories are conditioned by the perception and interpretation of the rememberer. They may or may not bear a close resemblance to what really happened, because what really happened is always subject to interpretation. Theologian Miroslav Volf puts it this way: "We are not just shaped *by* memories; we ourselves *shape* the memories that shape us."[1]

Memories are also flexible. "Memory," writes clinical psychologist Graham Lindegger, "is the process by which we organize our stored perceptions of our past life and experience."[2] But memory does not work like a video recording, in which the same images come up in the same order every time you play it. Rather, memory is more like a director interpreting a play. The play may be based upon an actual event, but each time the play is produced, it has a different feel, a different nuance, stemming from the director's interpretation. It is possible to reinterpret the narrative stream of one's memories; therapy and healing of memories build on this possibility. Memory is also a crucial element in the reconciliation of groups of people, as the truth commissions of the recent past have shown. But not just any memory will serve the cause of justice and integrity. Memories of past hurts also continually enflame present conflicts and wars.[3]

Memory is not only something that happens to us, then; it is also something we do. We can, to a certain degree, select which memories on which we choose to dwell. We can intentionally participate in memories that locate us in particular communities with particular identities. We can ritualize those memories as, for example, in the family stories we tell at funerals and memorials. Liturgy is, among other things, just such a ritualizing of memory.

Furthermore, memory is not simply about bringing the past into the present. Memory has an intrinsic relationship to hope in the future. Memories actually shape hopes, and hopes, in turn, influence memories. As we remember how things that appeared stuck actually did change, how we grew through our experiences, and how God worked in our lives in the past, we find it credible to hope that God can act again in our lives. Memories create a "horizon of expectation"[4] in which we live into the future. This relationship of memory to hope provides a key to its use in discernment.

Finally, memory not only connects the threads of our own life, but also connects our life with the lives of those around us. Benedictine author Joan Chittister helps us take memory from the personal to the social when she writes:

> The important things in life, one way or another, all leave us marked and scarred. We call it memory. We never stop remembering our triumphs. We never stop regretting our losses. Some of them mark us with bitterness. But all of them can, if we will allow them, mark us with wisdom. They transform us from our small, puny, self-centered selves into people of compassion. For the first time, we understand the fearful and the sinful and the exhausted. They have become us and we have become them as well. We recognize the down-and-out in the street who mirrors our despair. We commiserate with the anger of the marginalized. We identify with the invisibility of the outcast. We can finally hear the rage of the forgotten. We are transformed.[5]

Memory helps us dissolve the barriers of perception between "them" and "us," inviting us to find ourselves in the middle of the human family. This new perspective on memory, that it connects us to our shared human condition, can add a new element to our memory prayer: from this vantage point—right in the middle of the human family—what is it that God is inviting us to do with respect to the issue we are discerning?

MEMORY'S GIFTS TO DISCERNMENT

Because memory is connected to the shaping of identity and a "horizon of expectation," it is a powerful source for discernment. Memory offers two related but distinct gifts for discernment: it reviews our past experiences, providing wisdom for present decisions, and it helps us experience our life as held and surrounded by grace.

The first gift, wisdom to bring to the present decision, is highlighted in the practice Approaching Discernment through Memory. It comes from looking at past moments where God may have been at work in your life for what those experiences can offer with respect to your present issue. Let's examine in some detail two contrasting examples of how memory affected individual discernment.

Tom's company is downsizing and will eventually close. It is simply a matter of time before he receives a pink slip, as many of his less senior colleagues already have. He says that, although knowing that the end is coming might seem helpful—and, in some ways it is (no replacing the aging car right now, for example)—he is bothered by the uncertainty.

When will it come? What will he do then? How will he care for his family? Should he try to become one of the "gypsies" who move from plant to plant in the same company? Or should he try to retool and get out of this line of work altogether?

As Tom pays attention to his feeling of anxiousness, he recalls other times when he felt similar anxiety. One episode from his childhood stands out, when he was eight years old and his own father lost his job. This experience seemed to Tom to be a good candidate for the practice of Approaching Discernment through Memory. He begins by inviting God to be with him as he revisits the memory, and asks for the grace to understand how this memory can help him in his present quandary. Then, in the context of prayer, he returns to the memory and fills in details. He remembers as an eight-year-old being quite oblivious at first. He might not even have been aware of the implications of his father's job loss at all had he not seen his parents talking quietly long into the night, and his father's drawn face. He remembers thinking: *Something is really wrong. What can my dad do now? Will we have to move?* At first he swallowed his fear, but several days later it came tumbling out along with a lot of tears. When his parents realized how much of their anxiety he had taken in, they began to talk openly in front of him as they considered their various options. The parents' struggle became a family matter, and Tom's feelings and thoughts were attended. Within another week, they came to a plan: Tom's mother would take in laundry and altering, Tom would run errands in the neighborhood for his own spending money, and his dad would cross-train as a machinist, taking odd jobs on the weekends to boost the family's cash flow. The apprenticeship course took two years in those days, and another nine weeks went by before his dad landed another steady job. They were lean years, but together the family weathered the period. They often looked back at the struggle, marveling that they came through it together and stronger, if less well-off than they might have been if circumstances had not taken the turn they did.

As Tom fills in the details of this memory, he realizes that as soon as his eight-year-old self's anxiety was shared, it decreased. When the family together began to talk about the implications of his father's sudden job loss, he began to take pride in helping out for the good of the family. He remembers that his anxiety was transformed into a feeling of importance and even self-reliance. The sharing seemed to be the key to unlocking this transformation. Now that he is the one facing job loss, he's keeping his anxiety to himself much as his parents had done at first.

What would happen if he shared it judiciously with his children? What might they together come up with as a strategy for this in-between time? He resolves to talk this idea over with his wife.

He also remembers another time, a similar anxiety but different circumstance. He was just past his eighteenth birthday and waiting for his draft number to be drawn. Many of his friends were already in boot camp and probably on their way to Vietnam. He was feeling stuck as well as anxious, not wanting to start something he would have to drop abruptly. He remembers thinking, *I'm going nuts! I have to get out of the house.* He decided to round up all the neighborhood boys and organize a baseball team. By the time his number was drawn and he left for boot camp, the team had amassed a pretty good record playing the local parochial school teams. Even though none of their gear matched, they made up for their ragged appearance by their teamwork. Tom noticed that getting out of the house and doing something had helped him channel his anxiety into a constructive outcome—coaching the team was actually a satisfying challenge. In terms of his present anxiety, he realizes that rather than simply waiting for an ax to fall in the form of a pink slip, he can take some kind of action of his own. His next question then becomes: What action shall I take?

Tom's discernment receives two important points of clarification: he can judiciously share his anxiety about waiting, and he can find some action, however small, to invest in and thereby create some personal forward movement in the time of waiting. He is vaguely aware that he did not think of God having anything to do with either of these events when they happened, but from the perspective of his discernment, he is quite sure that God was actively at work in their family in that moment. Moreover, the memories that surface in his prayer offer him options that make him feel freer. If this feeling of freedom lasts, he has come to realize, it is an indication of the life of the Spirit in his everyday life. He knows he has more to do with the information that came to him from his memories, but he feels a certain amount of energy just in the possibilities. He closes the formal time of prayer with his own spontaneous prayer of gratitude, and picks up his journal to note the significant shifts and what he learned from this exercise.

In our second example, Kathy's approach to memory in discernment is much more cautious. She divides her life into before and after—before being sexually assaulted and after it. Although the assault was nearly three years ago, she still has flashbacks and nightmares. Because Kathy had worked with these negative and destructive memories in the context of her rape crisis support group, the traumatic memories have gradually lost some of their powerful hold on her. Other memories are beginning to surface, and this realization gives her the courage to approach the memory exercise, but still with appropriate safeguards. The solidarity of her support group has also helped her have the courage to remember when life was different and to hope that she will heal from this trauma and recover a different vision of life as a survivor rather than as a victim.

Kathy resolves to approach the memory prayer only in the confines of a safe space. She calls up her rape crisis counselor, Peggy, explains what she wants to do, and asks her to sit with her as she does the memory exercises. Peggy agrees, because she knows that Kathy is wise to have an outside person with some training to accompany her in this inner work. If the destructive memories start to overwhelm constructive ones, Peggy can reinforce the reality that Kathy is safe and is a precious child of God who is not ultimately defined by this single act of violence against her person. They meet on a Sunday afternoon for Kathy's memory exercise, and Peggy joins Kathy in her prayer. As memories surface in Kathy's prayer, she tells them to Peggy; getting these memories outside herself helps Kathy feel more control over their effects.

Kathy's experience reminds us that all memories are not benign. If a traumatic or destructive memory begins to overwhelm us, we need to stop the memory exercise. We may need to solicit outside help, as did Kathy, if we have reason to suspect that traumatic memories may surface.

Tom's and Kathy's very different experiences point us to the possibilities, limitations, and cautions of approaching discernment through memory. Their experiences are based on the psychological assumption that memory is the connective tissue that knits together the past, present, and future to create continuity in one's life and on the theological assumption that God has been present in every event of one's life and can work through a memory to reveal that presence and to offer guidance.

Memory's second gift to discernment is its ability to help us experience our life as held and surrounded by grace; this is the connection between memory and hope that we noticed earlier. Puritan John Bunyan understood this gift, writing in his autobiography, "It is profitable for Christians to be often calling to mind the very beginnings of Grace with their Souls. . . . Yea, look diligently, and leave no corner therein unsearched, for there is treasure hid, even the treasure of your first and second experience of the grace of God toward you."[6]

Through memory we can become aware of who we are before God, and who we are before God creates the expectation that God will continue to sustain us in the future as in the past. This "horizon of expectation" is the fruit of the first memory practice in chapter 2, Remembering Your Personal History. If you did not begin to experience this fruit earlier, now is a good time to stop and repeat that earlier spiritual practice, and see what grace God offers in the repetition.

Memory can also bring back particular experiences connected with biblical texts. I remember vividly a time many years ago as I was praying with the resurrection appearance of Jesus to Mary Magdalene. As my prayer unfolded, I had the distinct sense that Jesus was appearing to me, and I was recognizing who he really was. That text has not been the same for me since, having been personalized by my own religious experience, always available to my memory. Every time I hear that text, I renew the sense of being personally visited by the resurrected Christ and being warmed again by his personal presence.

MEMORY IN OUR BIBLICAL HERITAGE

Scripture gives us two particularly vivid and paradigmatic examples of the use of memory in shaping our understanding of God's continuing presence. The first one begins in the exodus event. Whoever the ragged group of Semites actually was who straggled out of Egypt and wandered around the desert of Sinai, the memory of this event was etched into the psyches of the Israelites' children and their children's children.

"Remember this day on which you came out of Egypt, out of the house of slavery, because the LORD brought you out from there by the strength of hand; no leavened bread shall be eaten. . . . When the LORD brings you into the land of the Canaanites, the Hittites, the Amorites, the Hivites, and the Jebusites, which he swore to your ancestors to give you, a land flowing with milk and honey, you shall keep this observance in this month. Seven days you shall eat unleavened bread, and on the seventh day there shall be a festival to the LORD. Unleavened bread shall be eaten for seven days; no leavened bread shall be seen in your possession, and no leaven shall be seen among you in all your territory. You shall tell your children on that day, 'It is because of what the LORD did for me when I came out of Egypt.' It shall serve for you as a sign on your hand and as a reminder on your forehead, so that the teaching of the LORD may be on your lips; for with a strong hand the LORD brought you out of Egypt. You shall keep this ordinance at its proper time from year to year."

(Exod. 13:3, 5–10)

All of the evangelists, in one way or another, place the final supper of Jesus with his apostles, and ultimately his death, in the context of that same Feast of Unleavened Bread. Echoing that first Passover from Egypt, Jesus leaves his followers the great Christian memorial action of the Eucharist. Luke underscores this link between memory and action: "Do this," Jesus says, "in memory of me." Paul offers the earliest recounting of the Eucharist narrative; he too wants to reinforce the power of memory: "For as often as you eat this bread and drink the cup, you proclaim the Lord's death until he comes" (1 Cor. 11:26). From this juxtaposition of enacted memories, it is but a small step for Christian Easter liturgies from earliest times to today to echo Paul in proclaiming: "For our paschal lamb, Christ, has been sacrificed. Therefore, let us celebrate the festival" (1 Cor. 5:7–8).

As we recognize the function of memory in the life of the Jewish and Christian communities, we can see a parallel way that memory can work in our own personal lives. Most of us have touchstone moments, moments of clarity in which God has visited us in a way that we could clearly apprehend at the time. Similar touchstone moments are recorded in Scripture: Matthew meeting Jesus and hearing a compelling "Follow me"; Saul being thrown from his horse on the way to Damascus, and realizing that it is Jesus himself that he had been persecuting as he zealously pursued Jesus' followers; Peter seeing a vision of food spread out in front of him and the invitation "Take and eat!" Most of us have had some moments where the mystery of God has broken through into our personal lives. However, if we have not done much with them, they recede in our consciousness until they become too diffuse to be of much help in discernment. Yet even just one such experience of God can serve us well in discernment. We can return to the qualities of that meeting with the Holy One—the freedom, the expansiveness, the courage, the energy, the peace, the other fruits—and use them as a kind of baseline, a paradigmatic experience of God to which we can compare and contrast other, less clear experiences that may occur in our discernment.[7]

Even as you are reading, you may be able to recall one such moment. Very likely, there are others. You can use the following simple practice to surface such moments in your own life:

Practice: Naming a Moment of Freedom

Memories of spiritual freedom bring us a special grace and serve an important role in discernment. They give us points of comparison for other memories: do these other memories also bring us spiritual freedom? This exercise guides you in remembering and reexperiencing a time of particular spiritual freedom.

1. Begin, as always, by preparing your body for relaxed attentiveness, and also gathering your concerns and then letting go of them for the duration of this time of prayer.

2. When you are sufficiently quiet, inside and outside, ask God for the grace you desire: to remember and reexperience a moment in which God was clearly present to you.

3. Allow such an encounter with Holy Mystery to surface, waiting for it without anxiety and with anticipation. If other kinds of memories surface, set them aside.

4. When a memory of an experience of God does come, recall the experience in detail. What was the quality of the freedom you experienced then? Reexperience that freedom now. Record it in your journal.

5. If possible, find a time to relate this experience and the quality of freedom to another person: a friend, spouse, pastor, or spiritual director, for example.

6. Give thanks to God for the grace God gave you at that moment.

5

Intuition's Knowing

Intuition offers its wisdom in its own way. Through it, we are able to gather information that already resides within us, but about which we are not yet aware. Intuition can be spontaneous, powerful, and convincing in uniting feeling and reason, will and action, or it can be a tiny, subtle nudge or hunch. It can propel us toward a decision and action.[1] Yet we always remain free to choose our response to the information offered to our discernment by intuition, and no matter how right an intuition may feel, it is important to reinforce and confirm intuitions through several other entry points and by the touchstones discussed in chapter 11. There is no need to commit yourself to act on your intuition, especially if you are somewhat distrustful of it. But, in conjunction with other modes of discernment, intuition can become a powerful carrier of inner wisdom, and for some persons, it is the primary way of approaching decisions.

In this chapter, we examine what intuition is, how it functions in discernment, and its biblical grounding. We also explore two examples from the Christian spiritual tradition that employ intuition in discernment, Ignatius of Loyola and the Religious Society of Friends (Quakers). The first and primary exercise, Approaching Discernment through Intuition, provides a guide to praying with intuition as part of your discernment. The second practice, Clearness Committee, offers a prayerful way, grounded in intuition, to involve a group in your discernment.

Practice: Approaching Discernment through Intuition

Accessing your intuition can be as simple as being quiet, patient, and welcoming. Your intuition may present hints about your call through images, sounds, colors, or other sensations registered in your body; in order to see the big picture, these clues need to be considered alongside those you receive from other entry points. Sometimes intuition offers a clear sense of exactly what's at stake and what you should do. Neither vague nor clear intuitions is better; they are just different. Welcome whatever comes, and then look at it in light of your desire to follow God's call as it unfolds.

1. Remind yourself that God can speak through your intuition. Offer to God this time of paying attention to the voice of your intuition. Ask specifically for the guidance of the Holy Spirit.

2. Become quiet, inside and outside. Rhythmic breathing may assist you in stilling yourself. Take as much time as you need. Allow your consciousness to be open to your depths.

3. Wait in openness. Does some option, sensibility, or sensation arrive whole, delivered to you as if from another? Describe it in your journal and then proceed to step 4.

OR

Permit images to float freely (they may or may not be visual). Write them down as they come to you, returning to the silence after each one. When the images or the sensations seem to stop, proceed to the next step.

4. Does one sensibility or gut feeling or image seem to embody the decision you face better than others? Which one(s) has a rightness? a freshness? an energy?

5. In your journal, write about what options this sensibility or gut feeling might suggest to you. What does a tentative decision look like in light of your intuition?

6. Return to your desire to follow God's call. Speak with God about what emerges from this process. Record the outcome of this prayer in your journal.

"I JUST KNOW IT"

Intuition is a kind of immediate knowing, without the conscious use of reason. We know far more than our conscious minds process; intuition collects data that is outside of our conscious awareness and presents it to our conscious mind for its consideration. This prayer is designed to help you become receptive to the information you receive through intuition.

Intuitions come in different ways to different people—through feelings ("I just don't feel right about this"), images ("I saw myself speaking comfortably before a large crowd—imagine me doing that!"), body sensations ("I have a gut feeling that I could work well with her," or "It was like a little voice in my ear saying 'Go for it!'"), or thoughts ("The whole plan just appeared in my mind all by itself"). What distinguishes intuition from sensations, thinking, or feeling is that intuitions just arrive, offering knowledge as if out of the blue. Be alert to the variety of ways that your intuitions might speak to you through this prayer.

Intuitions cannot necessarily be summoned up on command, and this practice may take place in stages over several days. Do not be disappointed if your intuition seems to offer you nothing during your time of prayer. Intuition is often accessed most successfully by indirection, appearing precisely when we are not directly looking for it—hence the flashes of insight that arrive in the shower or in the moments between waking and sleeping or when we are engaged in some mindless activity. Several days after your formal intuition prayer, a hunch may form that relates to your decision, or a dream may contain a suggestion that had not occurred to you during your reflection. Treat such bits of information as if they are intuitions for purposes of this discernment and spend some time with the final three steps of the practice in order to develop and relate them to the discernment process as a whole. This practice, then, may take place in stages over several days.

There are many ways to gain access to intuitions; don't be limited by the suggestions in the prayer exercise, but be creative in adapting and adding to the prayer. Drawing (especially with your nondominant hand), working clay, hearing or performing music, and dance are especially fruitful sources of intuitive wisdom. Intuitions can also arrive through other senses: touch, odors, colors, symbols. They also come through dreams; if you invite a dream, you may very well receive one.

Intuition can be useful even when you don't have a well-formed question. In fact, it may be good to start with this entry point when you have some sense that a decision might be on the horizon, but you can't yet formulate it very precisely. Intuition may provide you with clues that eventually lead to the heart of the matter in a way your rational mind or your affections are unable to do because they work at a completely different level of processing.

INTUITION IN THE CULTURE

Not everyone is comfortable with intuition. Some trust it, having found that these flashes of insight have proven helpful and sufficiently accurate, at least in certain situations. Others discount it as irrational. Actually, it is more accurate to say that intuition is nonrational. That is, although intuitions arrive without the aid of one's consciousness, they can be subject to verification and critique through our rational processes. Unfortunately, our culture tends to favor reason in decision making and decisions made on purely rational grounds, which can rule out the help that intuition offers for discernment.

In fact, intuition is part of knowing. Intuition furnishes the first experimental data, via hunches or educated guesses, that we can then test with reason. In a similar manner, it is also the source of the fundamental hunches that are the foundation of scientific experiments and even philosophical speculation—the famous aha moment where things come together in a way that seemed illogical—or a possibility that went unnoticed, but now seems obvious or at least plausible enough to investigate further. From the hunch, a theory is formulated and a research project set up to test the theory, as Jonas Salk observed:

> It is always with excitement that I wake up in the morning wondering what my intuition will toss up to me, like gifts from the sea. I work with it and rely on it. It's my partner. . . . When I worked on the polio vaccine, I had a theory. I guided each [experiment] by imagining myself in the phenomenon in which I was interested. The intuitive realm . . . guides my thinking. Intuition will tell the thinking mind where to look next.[2]

As we see in Salk's example, while intuition may grasp the significance of the data that comes to us through our senses, to bear its full fruit in our daily lives, it must be complemented by discursive reasoning, which can even include scientific research or philosophical and theological reflection.[3]

Some people are highly intuitive. In fact, the noun "intuitive," used as a synonym for "psychic," has come to describe people whose ability to "know without knowing" is so striking that it appears to be magical to the rest of us. The intuition process in this chapter does not rely on such psychic powers, however. In the exercise, you are simply allowing ordinary intuitions to be admitted as data for your discernment process. Furthermore, it is not wise to make any decision based solely on intuition. As with any of the entry points to discernment, the information that intuition gives you should be balanced with information gathered through other entry points into discernment, such as reason.

We can also look at intuition from a different perspective. The Myers-Briggs Type Indicator (MBTI),[4] a widely used instrument for assessing personality types, looks at intuition in light of the senses. Rather than contrasting intuition with thinking, the MBTI looks at where we glean the information that we then evaluate through thinking or feeling. Does it come to us from the exterior world, through our senses? Or does it come to us from our inner world, gleaned through intuition? About 65 percent of people prefer to base their judgments and decisions on the sense data that comes to them from the exterior world, a distinction in preferences the Myers-Briggs Type Indicator identifies as the difference between intuitive and sensate functions. Those who prefer the sensate function see the various trees in all their particularity, but those who prefer intuition see the forest whole, with all the interconnections that must exist to create "forest" from "trees." Sensate persons are very aware of concrete details, things in all their uniqueness. Intuitive persons tend to move from the thing (which they may not be able to describe well a few minutes later) to the interconnections that thing stimulates in their thinking, which *is* vivid. Sensate persons often demonstrate creativity by perfecting an idea or system already in existence, thinking up novel applications for it. Intuitive persons demonstrate creativity by imagining something that hasn't yet been considered. Sensate persons tend to think in linear fashion and prefer clear, logical proofs; intuitive persons frequently engage in leaps in thinking that may be difficult for others to follow and are intrigued by inferences, possibilities, and inner psychological dynamics. Sensate persons like practical ideas and commonsense solutions to problems, while intuitive persons prefer new ideas for their own sake and are more apt to look for an innovative solution to an old problem.[5]

Both of these ways of gathering and processing data, the sensate and the intuitive, are useful. We all have the ability to use both in discernment, but usually we have a clear preference for one over the other. In the next chapter we examine the sensate preferences and how they can assist our discernment as we examine how the body and our senses might offer information for our discernment process. As you pray with each way of gathering data, you may discover a decided preference for one over the other. If so, I encourage you to build it into your decision-making processes in the future. At the same time, don't completely overlook your less-preferred way of gathering information, as it will often allow you to discover something important that you might otherwise have overlooked.

BIBLICAL AND THEOLOGICAL GROUNDING

As the creator and source of our life, God speaks in the deep impulses of the soul. Intuition is one way that we can receive this deep truth from within about life's direction. Although the biblical authors lacked the modern notion of intuition, we find examples and theological explanations for the immediate knowing that we today call intuition.

Biblical writers assume without question that God revealed Godself in many ways, including through silence, dreams, visions, direct speech, and infused virtues, gifts, and powers. The resulting knowledge was understood to come from God, who was to be served through its use. For example, in Daniel 1:17 we read, "To these four young men God gave knowledge and skill in every aspect of literature and wisdom; Daniel also had insight into all visions and dreams." If the knowledge came directly without the ordinary learning processes, a plausible interpretation of this text, it would describe what we speak of today as intuition.

Numbers 12:6–8 provides another example of God's communication. Relatively early in their long sojourn in the desert of Sinai, when the Israelites and their leader Moses were just learning how to survive and be tempered by God into God's people, tensions arose between Moses, Aaron, and Miriam about who might speak for the Lord. The Lord promptly makes very clear that, while there are many prophets with whom God communicates through visions and dreams, Moses has a more privileged access, for he sees God face to face.

> "When there are prophets among you,
>   I the LORD make myself known to them in visions;

I speak to them in dreams.
Not so with my servant Moses;
 he is entrusted with all my house.
With him I speak face to face—clearly, not in riddles;
 and he beholds the form of the LORD."

While the dreams and visions are clearly God's revelation, they are like riddles to be solved—like much of what comes through intuition. But when God speaks directly to Moses, this ambiguity disappears.

In 1 Kings 19, silence is the context of immediate knowing. After Elijah was fed in the desert, he was directed to travel forty days and forty nights to Horeb, the mountain of God. Here he was instructed to go out and stand on the mountain before the Lord as the Lord passed by. But the Lord was not manifested through the signs that, in that culture, would be expected to surround divine speech: mountain-crushing wind, earthquake, or fire. Instead, God's revelation is signaled through silence and received in reverent inner attention.

We find an account of revelation through a dream in 1 Kings 3. At the beginning of Solomon's reign, the Lord tells Solomon, "Ask what I should give you." Solomon, protesting that he is only a little child who "[does] not know how to go out or come in" compared to his father David, asks for an understanding mind, and particularly for the ability to discern between good and evil, in order to wisely govern God's people. God is pleased with this request, focused as it is on Solomon's service to the community, and grants Solomon not only a wise and discerning heart but also what he did not ask for: riches, honor, and a long life if he continues to walk in the way of the Lord.

Dreams also pepper Matthew's infancy narrative. Joseph's dream instructed him to take Mary and the child to Egypt, causing them to flee ahead of Herod's soldiers. The magi were likewise warned in a dream to return by another route, giving the little family a head start to safety. An angel returned to Joseph in yet another dream with the message that it was now safe to return home. Are these intuitions in the form of day or night dreams? Clearly, the biblical writer intends to show God revealing Godself directly. From Joseph's point of view, the communication arrives directly from another, whom, from his faith perspective, he understands to be trustworthy—to be, in fact, an angel of the Lord.

Isaiah 11 begins with a poetic description of the shoot from the stump of Jesse. The spirit of the Lord will endow this descendant of Jesse with the spirits of wisdom, understanding, and knowledge, among other gifts. Paul expands this list in 1 Corinthians 12:4–11, adding prophecy, the discernment of spirits, and interpretation of various kinds of tongues. These gifts work in an out-of-the-ordinary way and as a direct result of the Spirit, and Paul exhorts the community to use them to build up the whole community in Christ. Are these forms of divine revelation a type of intuition? Christian communities at various points have held this interpretation.

Theologians and spiritual writers continued to ponder God's communication in the postbiblical world. For example, medieval theologians tried to explain how it was that we came to know. Thomas Aquinas held that an intuitive act of intellectual knowledge (he assumed other kinds of knowledge existed) is, by its nature, the most perfect act of knowledge, since it is an immediate grasp of concrete reality. Indeed, he argued, the beatific vision consists precisely in this kind of immediate apprehension and direct knowing without conscious thinking and processing.[6] Some Christian mystics have maintained that the immediate knowing of God is possible in this life through contemplative experience. Thomas Merton put it this way: "In the depths of contemplative prayer there seems to be no division between subject and object, and there is no reason to make any statement either about God or about oneself. He IS and this reality absorbs everything else."[7] That is, we can intuitively grasp God's reality, even when our rational processes stumble in their explanations.

Two other examples from the Christian spiritual tradition show that the Christian understanding of illumination via intuition has continued to develop. An experience of Ignatius of Loyola illustrates the direct divine illumination reminiscent of biblical wisdom. In reminiscences recounted in the third person, Ignatius describes one particularly formative moment:

> Once he was going out of devotion to a church situated a little more than a mile from Manresa; I believe it is called St. Paul's and the road goes by the river. As he went along occupied with his devotions, he sat down for a little while with his face toward the river, which ran down below. While he was seated there, the eyes of his understanding began to be opened; not that he saw any vision, but he understood and learnt many things, both spiritual matters and matters of faith and of scholarship, and this with so great an enlightenment that everything seemed new to him.[8]

Even many years later, Ignatius takes pains to note that his revelation was so intense and so clear that it outweighed all his subsequent work at understanding, including years of theological study. As with the biblical figures cited above, Ignatius assumed that his revelation arrived directly from God. Also like the biblical precedents, he understood it was to be used apostolically—in his case, to guide his catechizing.

Today the Religious Society of Friends (Quakers) may represent the most refined spiritual use of intuition in the Christian tradition. This chapter's second intuition-oriented spiritual practice, the Clearness Committee, grew out of Quaker worship and decision making. Because the practice itself is so simple and spare, some historical and descriptive background helps unlock the depth of the practice.

Quakers have developed a way to encourage and understand the immediate intuitive reception of divine revelation that they call "leadings" or "openings." The Quaker Meeting for Worship consists of silent, worshipful attention. Occasionally someone receives a leading and speaks it out loud into the silence; then the meeting slips back into deep, worshipful silence. These leadings are understood to be the direct experience of the Source or as being taught by the Christ within.

Quakers govern themselves out of the same profound silence and reliance on direct revelation. Their unique system of governance attempts to eliminate the notions of majority and minority by allowing a unity to arise out of the silence and openings. When the clerk (chair) senses this unity present, he or she speaks the "sense of the meeting," and it is recorded as the decision of the group: no votes, no passionate arguments, no filibuster, no position papers, no minority reports.[9]

But not everything offered by intuition is from the divine. Over their more than three hundred years, Quakers have developed wisdom with which to help people understand what they are experiencing and judge if it is a true leading from the divine. A helpful example for our purposes is the idea that an individual's leadings to do certain things are also discerned by the community. John Woolman (1720–1772), the famous Quaker abolitionist, recounts such an experience in his journal:

> I then wrought at my trade as a tailor, carefully attended meetings for worship and discipline, and found an enlargement of gospel love in my mind and therein a concern to visit Friends in some of the back settlements of Pennsylvania and Virginia. And being thoughtful about a companion, I expressed it to my beloved friend Isaac Andrews, who then told me that he had drawings there and also to go through Maryland, Virginia and Carolina. After considerable time passed and several conferences with him, I felt easy to

accompany him throughout, if way opened for it. I opened the case in our Monthly Meeting and Friends expressing their unity therewith, we obtained certificates to travel as companions—his from Haddonfield [Meeting] and mine from Burlington [Meeting].[10]

Notice Woolman's "opening," the time spent he spent personally testing his sense of what he is being led to do, his subsequent consulting, and his awaiting the Meeting's confirmation, permission, and support. The practice of the Religious Society of Friends gives us some important clues not only about how to access our own leadings, but also how to test the information offered by intuition: we receive the intuition, ponder it prayerfully, and consult and complete the discernment in community.

Quakers originally used a Committee for Clearness to help persons drawn to marriage to discern in the context of the Meeting if they were called to this significant life decision. Usually, on hearing the word "committee," we think of an ad hoc group working on a particular task. In fact, a Clearness Committee is much closer to a contemplative faith-sharing group, designed to uphold you while you access your inner wisdom about a decision. It is particularly helpful if you face a major decision in which you want to be supported by a faith community.

To incorporate this spiritual practice into your own discernment, you will need to convene a group of five or six trusted individuals who are able to spend up to four hours over one or two sittings (though it may not take so long). You might ask members of a prayer group, friends from church, or other persons who understand and have some personal acquaintance with spirituality and will be able to approach the process in faith. They need not think like you or like each other; in fact, diversity in the group is a decided advantage.

A Quaker conviction guides this process: "there is that of God in every person." The Clearness Committee helps you to uncover "that of God"—God working through your own intuitive wisdom—already present within you with respect to your discernment issue. The committee's role is simple but difficult: to ask questions that will help you uncover your own intuitive wisdom. Their questions should be brief, honest, and caring. They should not be disguised advice, speeches, or storytelling. The questions need not elicit only logical and rational responses; some of the most useful questions may seem a bit "off the wall."[11] Nor need the questions be directly about your situation or your decision; if a question seems important to ask, a committee member is free to ask it.

Two committee members have particular functions. The clerk (chair) opens and closes the Clearness Committee, sets the worshipful tone, and serves as a kind of contemplative traffic cop, regulating the flow and pace of questions and assuring that all who wish to speak can do so. The recording clerk takes notes about what is said (questions and answers) and gives them to you for continued reflection. You are thus free to focus on answering the questions in the moment and also to ponder further once the group disperses.

As the discerner, you also have a task: to answer each question prayerfully and thoughtfully. However, you are always in charge of how deeply or whether you will answer a particular question aloud. It is a good idea to keep your responses relatively brief, so that more questions can be covered in the allotted time.

Participants should be prepared for lots of silence between questions. Much of the intuitive work goes on in the silence, so all parties should resist the temptation to fill the silence quickly with another question. In fact, questioners should wait a bit longer than feels comfortable to them, because the pacing feels much more intense to the person—you— answering the questions. If the pace feels too quick or intense, ask that it slow down. Finally, the committee members should agree that the written and oral parts of the process are bound by confidentiality.

Practice: Clearness Committee[12]

1. Choose the committee. Name a clerk (chair) and recording clerk (secretary). Set up the time and place for the group meeting, assuring at least two uninterrupted hours.

2. Before the meeting, write up your situation and the decision facing you, in about four to six pages. Be as concise as possible while still including relevant background factors and your hunches about what lies ahead. Distribute this summary to the members of the committee in advance of your meeting.

3. Convene the group as previously planned. The clerk clarifies all the roles and reminds the participants about confidentiality. Then all assembled move into some time of sustained silence, a time of expectant waiting and prayer.

4. When you feel focused and ready, summarize aloud the situation and the decision you are facing.

5. The committee members then ask you questions at a gentle and respectful pace.

6. Answer questions as they are asked. These questions—and your answers—point the way to the wisdom surrounding your issue.

7. At the conclusion of about two hours, or when you feel finished for this session, you may choose to ask the committee members what they observe, or you may wish simply to thank the members and allow the clerk to close the meeting. If you wish another session, you may request it at this time.

8. Prayerfully reflect on the entire experience. Further clarity may surface after the conclusion of the group sessions.

There are many possible responses to the two exercises in this chapter. Sometimes a breakthrough occurs and the way forward appears, but often we are left with little clues, hunches, a dream to work with, sometimes a metaphor or an image. Sometimes the gifts the intuition has to offer are yet to appear; be alert to them in the next days, taking care to bring them more formally into your prayer, using, for example, steps 3–6 of the practice Approaching Discernment through Intuition. Noting all the seemingly random bits of data in your discernment journal will help you connect the various dots offered by your intuition and between this entry point and others. If you started with only a vague sense of what's at stake, you may now have a better sense of a specific issue or question. If so, try reformulating your discernment issue using the practice Framing Your Discernment Question in chapter 3. But let the buyer beware: the opposite may happen! You may now realize, having accessed wisdom from your unconscious, that the issue is far broader and deeper than you originally suspected. Sometimes the discernment path is straight, and sometimes it is meandering. It really doesn't matter which, since wherever the path goes, we go there with God.

6

Body's Awareness

The body is a powerful carrier of wisdom. Everything we have experienced lives on in the body. Indeed, the body *is* life as we know it. Our senses registering the world, our muscles carrying our body, the digestive system breaking food into nourishment—this is the body at work. Our activities, people living together, tending to children, making love, falling ill, and dying—these, too, are our embodied selves acting in the world. All experience, and hence, all data for discernment, must come to us first through our bodies. Can listening to our bodies give us wisdom about the decision before us? If so, in what language does the body speak?

In this chapter, you will learn to notice and interpret the wisdom your body holds about how God is calling you in your discernment. We explore our often-ambivalent relationship to our bodies, look at some scriptural perspectives on embodiment, and learn how to listen more deeply to the body. There are three exercises: the first, Approaching Discernment through the Body, provides the basic discernment practice; Knowing Whose You Are links bodiliness to Scripture; and Focusing teaches how to access deeper wisdom from your body. Whether the body is an especially fruitful entry point for you or you are just beginning to pay attention to your body's wisdom, you can grow in your ability to receive wisdom from your body. Focusing, in particular, can help beginners and those more skilled in listening to their bodies access deeper levels of the wisdom it holds.

In this chapter, I introduce the terms "felt sense" and "body sense." The phrases are interchangeable and refer to internal bodily awareness, literally, the body's registering a sense of a particular problem, situation, or experience. These sensations can be quite subtle and take some practice to notice and learn to interpret—or, like the headache I typically get when my computer breaks down, they can be glaringly obvious. Still, unless their revelatory power is taken seriously, the wisdom they offer goes unclaimed.

This entry point on the body follows intuition because they provide an interesting contrast to each other; however, there is no reason that you need to use them in this order for your discernment. But in whatever order you use the various entry points, do bring the results of all your previous prayer with you as you begin a new entry point. With each additional exercise, the information becomes richer, and eventually patterns will begin to form. Some things will fade in importance, while others grow in significance. All the while, you are listening to God's call as it comes through the various exercises.

Practice: Approaching Discernment through the Body

If your body could talk, what would it say to you about your discernment? This prayer sets up a dialogue between you and your body. The language your body will use is the sensations that arise as you do the exercise. I refer to these sensations as "felt sense" or "body sense." Does adrenalin hit your bloodstream and fill you with energy? Perhaps your stomach knots up. Your shoulders may tense up or relax; you may frown or smile. Are you filled with a sense of well-being or with a vague foreboding that locates itself somewhere in your body? These are examples of body senses. When, in step 5, the directions invite you into a dialogue with your body, you might say to your body, for example, "Would it feel different if I got someone to help me instead of trying to do it by myself?" We begin, as we do all discernment prayer, by renewing our desire to meet God through our discernment.

1. Prayerfully renew your desire to follow God's call. Ask God to let this desire itself be more important than any specific outcome. If at any time you find your spiritual freedom fading, return to this prayer. Repeat it as often as necessary to help you remain indifferent to any particular outcome.

2. Clear a space inside you. Allow yourself to become aware of your body, all its parts and organs. Notice the blood flowing and the muscles going about their work, your organs functioning without you attending to them.

3. While attentive to your body and its responses, present to it your discernment question in some detail and pay attention to everything that happens in your body as you do.

4. What do you sense in your body with respect to your question? What is the quality of the felt sense? Write it out in your journal in some detail.

5. Carry on a dialogue with your body about your discernment question. If your body sense shifts, follow where it takes you.

6. Ask this body sensation what message it might bring about a decision. Record any new awareness about a potential decision that comes through your body.

7. Return to your desire to follow God's call. Place your new awareness before God and notice what happens. Record this outcome, too.

THE BODY AS A SOURCE OF REVELATION

I believe the body is an avenue into the wisdom we seek in discernment, and that we can access wisdom coming through the body as part of our prayerful approach to decision making. I do not know, however, if you found this exercise easy or difficult. Both responses are common. On the positive side, I've had people say, "I was pretty skeptical about having a conversation with my body. It seemed so hokey. But I tried it, and, you know, it worked!" I've also heard, "I had no idea that my body had an opinion at all so I was quite surprised that there was a definite shift in my body as I posed different possibilities."

Perhaps you made some discoveries as a result of the exercise. Sometimes people register surprise that their body may not be in sync with their mind: "My body says the opposite from my head, and now I have to think about what that might mean." Or, equally possible: "My body and my head are pointing to the same decision!" And some express delight that their bodies are included in discernment: "I always know what to do because I feel it in my body, so it's natural to pray this way."

Incorporating the body into discernment and calling on its wisdom can call up various responses. There is no correct response to this exercise. If you have a hard time noticing that anything at all is going on, it may be that you have not been in the habit of paying attention to your body, let alone pondering what it might suggest for discernment. Practice, perhaps using the Focusing exercise presented later in the chapter, will help you tune into your body.

But perhaps you had the opposite experience: maybe you were flooded with bodily sensations, even to the point of being overwhelmed by them. Some highly sensitive people receive body clues from everything that happens, which can burden them with too much detail. For some people, focusing on the body unlocks a trauma that has been stored there, out of their consciousness. Something as simple as a particular smell can bring the memory of the trauma rushing back. Emotional healing from traumas is not always as straightforward as physical healing. Memories of the trauma may still be carried with the tissues and neurons, and in this situation, healing often needs skilled assistance and accompaniment. For discernment, being able to control the speed or intensity of bodily sensations is key to using them fruitfully. If for any reason you are uncomfortable doing this exercise—or any of the others in this book—stop. Or do them only in a place and with people with whom you feel safe, as Kathy did when approaching the memory exercises in chapter 4.

FRIEND OR FOE? OUR OFTEN AMBIVALENT RELATIONSHIP TO OUR BODIES

Bodies matter in discernment. They are the sources of our unique selves, somehow bounded by our skin, and, at the same time, our deepest means of connection to others. As infants we learn who we are by touching and tasting and smelling the world around us, getting a sense of how much space we take up, how to move in that space, and how to relate to others who enter that space. Babies very early lock their eyes on their parents and caregivers, using their gaze to pull them into relationship. As we grow older we continue forming identity and relationship at more sophisticated levels. Our sex begins to shape our gender identity, and our gender identity shapes our relationships. By means of our bodies we range farther from home and parents, exploring a wider and wider world, experimenting, connecting, breaking away, repeating the sequence again and again. Stephanie Paulsell describes the paradox in which we live with our bodies, a paradox of being both bound by and being in relationship through one's body:

> [O]ur bodies exist both in relation to other bodies and in the integrity of their own boundedness. Even in the most intimate of relationships, secrets can be kept, held in the body. Even in the most intimate of relationships, one can never know fully the inner life of another nor can one share another's bodily experiences. . . . But even though our bodies are distinct from the bodies of those closest to us, it is through our bodies that we are also able to enter into relationship with others. . . . Everything depends on how those relations are formed—with gentleness or cruelty, attention or disdain.[1]

Bodily experience is inherently ambiguous. We live in the tension between being a body and having a body, between integrity and relationality, freedom and constraint, and sacredness and vulnerability.[2] At one moment, perhaps at the peak of physical exertion, we can experience our selves as all together and integrated in our bodies, but at another, perhaps at the diagnosis of a chronic or terminal illness, our body itself can appear to be the enemy. Yet one's whole self includes one's body, and in order to move toward wholeness, the body must neither be ignored nor denigrated nor overindulged.

You might concede that bodies in general may be holy but still not be comfortable with your own body as a source of God's revelation. Perhaps that body has been wounded, abused, even tortured. Perhaps you yourself have ignored it or abused it through immoderate use of food, drugs, or sensual pleasures. Perhaps you have suffered chronic illness or sudden loss of function of some part of your body. The truth is, it's pretty easy to see bodies as a general category as good—after all, God created bodies—even as *my* particular body, tied intimately to my sense of who I am, does not appear good or even acceptable. So how could my body be a means through which God speaks? The same Paul who gave us the metaphor of the body of Christ himself wrestled with his body: "For I delight in the law of God in my inmost self, but I see in my members another law at war with the law of my mind, making me captive to the law of sin that dwells in my members. Wretched man that I am! Who will rescue me from this body of death?" (Rom. 7:22–24).

The Christian tradition is filled with examples of practices that, while they seem as if they would constrain the body, at their best, actually lead to deeper freedom. Fasting as a spiritual practice, for example, can help us prepare an unencumbered space for attending to God and connect us viscerally with those who do not have sufficient food. Clothing the body modestly teaches us to respect our own bodies and those of others. Praying for indifference can free us to move to act for justice when it is risky. Refraining from the incessant demand of instant communications can remind us who is God and refresh us for our work on the morrow. Unfortunately, practices like sexual abstinence, dietary rules, Sabbath keeping, and fasting have sometimes been stressed in such a way or to such a degree that they communicate, not the spiritual freedom that is their goal, but a denigration of the body that leads to the opposite of this freedom. And yet, some boundedness and discipline is essential to developing an appropriate sense of self, competence and co-responsibility. We must also hold this tension between freedom and constraint in dynamic balance, neither too much freedom or the wrong kind of freedom, nor too much constraint or the wrong kind of constraint. Finding that balance takes constant discernment.

The tension between sacredness and vulnerability is most visible when we receive or give care for bodies at their most vulnerable moments. Taking my frail mother's feet into my hands and carefully and gently massaging them with delicately scented oil never failed to bring tears to my eyes. I was holding and honoring the feet that walked so many steps caring for me, my brothers, and so many other people, feet that could scarcely carry her any longer. Paulsell reflects on feet washing as her illustration of the dynamic tension between sacredness and vulnerability: "When you offer your feet to another to be washed and gently dried, it is impossible not to notice the difficult relationship between our bodies and our identities. And when you kneel to wash the feet of another, you glimpse the vulnerabilities that attention to the body can evoke."[3]

SCRIPTURE ON THE BODY

Since many people in our culture experience an ambivalent relationship to their bodies that hinders discernment, it is important to become comfortable with one's body as a means of prayerful encounter with the Living One. Scripture can guide us in this task; it is filled with bodies and bodiliness.

Recall how Genesis speaks poetically about the sweep of creation. God's creative "Let there be" (Gen. 1) brings forth the bodies of an immense variety of living things, Adam (human being) among them, made in God's own image. This creation, all of it, God judged to be very good. The second creation account (Gen. 2–3) details the fashioning of a particular body, Eve's. It also seeks to account for the imperfection, struggle, and violence that humans incur precisely in their embodied selves. Clearly the ambiguity about bodies has been with us since the dawn of creation.

The exodus, the decisive event that formed the people of Israel, is remarkably physical. Moses' attention is caught by a fiery bush that doesn't burn up, by voices that command and guide him. A plague kills the firstborn of animals and humans. The angel of death passes over only those marked by the sign of the covenant, blood from the paschal sacrifice. The Israelites flee through a watery place that is unaccountably dry under their feet; then turn and watch that same sea close over the Egyptian army, drowning them and all their horses and charioteers. They are sustained in the desert by gathering just enough manna and quail for the day's food, unable to preserve and carry any for the next. And none could miss the thunder that accompanied God's voice as God gave them the Law, or the cloud that guided them by day and the fire by night. This God of the Israelites was indeed a God who communicated with the chosen people in ways their senses could apprehend.

Perhaps the greatest celebration of the body in the Scriptures is the Song of Solomon. An unabashed love poem, it begins, "Let him kiss me with the kisses of his mouth!" While interpreters have not always known what to do with this text, perhaps out of their own discomfort, the body is certainly honored in its lovely descriptions of sexual desire!

> How beautiful you are, my love,
>   how very beautiful!
> Your eyes are doves
>   behind your veil.
> Your hair is like a flock of goats,
>   moving down the slopes of Gilead.
> Your teeth are like a flock of shorn ewes
>   that have come up from the washing,
> all of which bear twins,
>   and not one among them is bereaved.
> Your lips are like a crimson thread,

and your mouth is lovely.
Your cheeks are like halves of a pomegranate
    behind your veil. . . .
Your two breasts are like two fawns,
    twins of a gazelle,
    that feed among the lilies.

(Song 4:1–3, 5)

In the Gospels, we encounter the mystery that God became fully present in a particular human body, in a particular family dwelling in a small town of an unremarkable Roman colony. Toward the end of his life, Jesus preached to the crowds and gathered about him a group of twelve, whom he taught in greater depth, often with homey parables about seeds, weeds, coins, and sheep. On the night before he died, he tended to the bodies of his closest friends by washing their feet; this is how they were to behave when he was gone. In their final supper together, he left them bread broken and cup poured out, food to sustain their spirits and their community in the days to come when he would no longer be with them. His death at the hands of the Roman colonizers, a death agitated for by the religious leaders of his own country, seemed to dash the hopes of his followers that indeed he was the long-awaited Messiah. But rumors that he had appeared to them were confirmed: "Please give me something to eat," he said after greeting them. "Please touch my hands and feet and side," he said to Thomas. He meant them to know for sure that it was really his body, not some kind of ghost. The Fourth Gospel concludes with Jesus cooking breakfast for all his disciples, worn out from a night of fishing, the final story in a Gospel that begins "The Word became flesh and lived among us . . . full of grace and truth" (John 1:14).

The body supplied one of Paul's most fruitful metaphors: the church as the body of Christ. But the body is more than a metaphor; our physical bodies matter. God dwelt among us as one like us in all things except sin (Heb. 4:16), in a body like ours. We are commanded to care for our bodies, putting to death all that is earthly—fornication, impurity, passion, evil desire, and greed, clothing ourselves instead with compassion, kindness, humility, meekness, patience, and, above all, love (Col. 3:5–12). This way of discipleship is both practical and embodied, as we see in this admonition from the Letter of James: "If a brother or sister is naked and lacks daily food, and one of you says to them, 'Go in peace; keep warm and eat your fill,' and yet you do not supply their bodily needs, what is the good of that?" (Jas. 2:15–16). Indeed, bodies matter in God's design, especially the bodies of those most vulnerable.

My body makes me uniquely who I am. I matter to God. You matter to God. We conclude our brief survey of the treatment of the body in Scripture with a guided meditation that invites you to deepen your connection to our God, to bring all of yourself to God, to see yourself as God sees you, to ground your experience of body-self in God's own word addressed to you personally. Since this meditation is not directly related to your discernment process, it can be done at any time. But if you found Approaching Discernment through the Body difficult, this practice may help you be more comfortable with using your body in discernment.

Practice: Knowing Whose You Are[4]

Psalm 139 forms the basis of this guided meditation. If you are praying in a group, the psalm may be read by one voice and the reflection by another voice. Be sure to leave ample time for reflection at the places signaled by the ellipses. In using this meditation in your own personal prayer, you may find it helpful to record the psalm and the reflections and play the tape as you do this exercise. You can then close your eyes and hear the psalm, and pause as long and where you want, all without being tied to the printed text.

> O LORD, you have searched me and known me.
> You know when I sit down and when I rise up;
>   you discern my thoughts from far away.
> You search out my path and my lying down,
>   and are acquainted with all my ways.

(You are known, intimately. . . . How does it feel to be so totally known? A relief? Frightening? Exciting? . . . Do you want to move toward the Knower? Or find some safety in which to hide? . . . Does it matter to you who it is who knows you? . . .)

> You hem me in, behind and before,
>   and lay your hand upon me.

(The experience of being known is like a fence, but is it a fence which provides security or keeps you bound? Or perhaps is it, paradoxically, both?)

Such knowledge is too wonderful for me;
    it is so high that I cannot attain it.

(Rest in this paradox. . . .)

Where can I go from your spirit?
    Or where can I flee from your presence?
If I ascend to heaven, you are there;
    if I make my bed in Sheol, you are there.
If I take the wings of the morning
    and settle at the farthest limits of the sea,
even there your hand shall lead me,
    and your right hand shall hold me fast.
If I say, "Surely the darkness shall cover me,
    and the light around me become night,"
even the darkness is not dark to you;
    the night is as bright as the day,
    for darkness is as light to you.

(Do you want to run from this intimacy? . . . Rest in it? . . . Let the freedom that can come from being totally known by a loving, merciful God seep gradually into your being. . . . Nothing to hide, no need for pretense, no need to be anything other than exactly who you are . . .)

For it was you who formed my inward parts;
    you knit me together in my mother's womb.
I praise you, for I am fearfully and wonderfully made.
    Wonderful are your works;
that I know very well.
    My frame was not hidden from you,
when I was being made in secret,
    intricately woven in the depths of the earth.
Your eyes beheld my unformed substance.
In your book were written
    all the days that were formed for me,
    when none of them as yet existed.

(God's love for you is infinitely greater than the love that parents have for their children. . . . Reflect on the deep connection between you and God. . . .)

How weighty to me are your thoughts, O God!
    How vast is the sum of them!
I try to count them—they are more than the sand;
    I come to the end—I am still with you.

(Let the psalmist's wonder grow in you too. . . .
But, there are violent parts to us; these too are known.)

O that you would kill the wicked, O God,
    and that the bloodthirsty would depart from me—
those who speak of you maliciously,
    and lift themselves up against you for evil!
Do I not hate those who hate you, O LORD?
    And do I not loathe those who rise up against you?
I hate them with perfect hatred;
    I count them my enemies.

(Can you bring even these parts of yourself to God? . . . Can you
admit to yourself what God already knows? . . . Can you allow God
to work in you at your points of greatest weakness? . . . Can you let
God work any justice that is necessary?)

Search me, O God, and know my heart;
    test me and know my thoughts.
See if there is any wicked way in me,
    and lead me in the way everlasting.

(Amen . . . So be it. . . .)

LISTENING TO THE LANGUAGE OF THE BODY

In the 1970s, psychotherapist and researcher Eugene Gendlin began to ask why some psychotherapy worked and some brought no results at all. He eventually concluded that only the body "knows" where the crux of the person's problem actually lies, and when persons actually do change, it registers in the body. After more experimentation, he realized that it was possible for people to learn to read their body's cues in order to participate in their own healing and transformation. A process he called Focusing,[5] the short form of which I will adapt below, was the result of his years of research. It wasn't long before some Christian spiritual directors, already convinced of the goodness of the body through their reflections on Scripture and the Christian spiritual tradition, began to realize that Gendlin's work pointed out an important avenue for discernment.[6] This chapter's first exercise, Approaching Discernment through the Body, incorporates Gendlin's basic approach, listening to the body for its cues, which, for our use in discernment, center around options contained in the discernment. Since many contemporary persons struggle to incorporate the body into their spirituality at all, let alone into their discernment, Gendlin's Focusing may offer a way to develop the ability to read the important cues from one's body. If Focusing helps you learn to sense and interpret these cues, by all means practice the listening it leads you through; if it just seems confusing, feel free to ignore it—as with all the supplementary exercises in this book.

Focusing incorporates six steps, each of which can lead to an actual physical change in one's body. At the same time, the original problem, issue, or, in our case, discernment question, also shifts, however subtly. It is possible, then, to trace the process of change by reading the shifts in one's body, and—important for discernment—to get a sense of which option will be better for us than another.

Earlier in the chapter, I described a felt sense or a body sense as an internal body awareness, as your body's sense of a particular experience. The term was actually coined by Gendlin. He found that it is not the therapist's technique that determines the success of psychotherapy, but something the patient does. Without exception, persons who made progress in their therapy intuitively focused inside themselves on a very subtle and vague internal bodily awareness—the experience Gendlin called a felt sense and used it to guide them forward in their therapy. Since the same body guidance can work with any issue, including those posed by discernment, body guidance can also assist us in our discernment.

This felt or body sense, Gendlin points out, is not an emotion, which we could more readily recognize. Emotions also reside in the body, but the felt sense is more basic than emotions. We usually know when we are happy, sad, angry, or wistful, for example, but a felt sense, because it lacks such an emotional resonance, may elude detection at first. The felt sense can feel meaningful, but not quite known.[7] It might register, for example, as an ache, a twitch, a tension, or an even more vague lightness or heaviness. It's the lack of explicit language that makes reading the body a challenge, and Focusing can help us learn how to listen for and put into words these subtle experiences.

A felt sense forms as a person pays attention to everything that clusters around some situation (for us, the discernment question). As people turn their attention to this as-yet-unarticulated knowing, they eventually find some words that express both what is happening in the body and, at another step, new insights into the situation. Once we can put some language around these felt senses, we can then share them with another, ponder their meaning, and eventually make decisions about what they tell us.

Actually, Focusing can assist with discerning decisions at several levels. In addition to the help that it offers in becoming acquainted with our own felt senses and how to read them, it may also reveal things that the body says must be dealt with before we can be free enough to consider the discernment question. Remember Pete, whom we met in chapter 3 trying to discern which college he would attend? One of the scenarios I posed then—we were discussing the significance of the assumptions we bring to discernment—was the possibility that Pete is not called to school at all right now. How might such a scenario unfold using Focusing? Suppose, as Pete continued into his discernment about which college he would attend, he became aware that he never mustered up enthusiasm for any of the schools he was considering. Through Focusing, following a vague sense of dis-ease sensed at first as lack of energy, he might realize, for example, that all options for college left him not only with lack of energy. As he continued to listen to his body, he might eventually describe his body sense of his situation as a "catch in his throat." Equally important, he notices that his throat is completely relaxed when he is not considering school. If Pete took this clue from his body seriously, he might come to the conclusion that his discernment is focused on the wrong question. Maybe school is not God's call for him at this moment. He could then change his discernment question from "What college shall I attend?" to "Am I being called to attend college at this point?" Although I did not formally use Focusing steps to help discern my response to the job interview I described in chapter 3 (I didn't know about Focusing then!), I was intuitively reading the continually reappearing knot in my stomach as an indication that my discernment question, "Shall I accept this position if it is offered?" should be answered negatively.

If you feel sufficiently comfortable with Focusing, you might use it as a major aspect of your discernment. In that case, simply substitute your discernment question for every place that the Focusing directions use the word "problem." Focusing can also be a part of the confirmation process that we will discuss more thoroughly in chapter 11: does the body itself say yes to the outcome of discernment?

Practice: Focusing[8]

Your goal in this exercise is to listen to the wisdom your body can reveal about the problem, issue, or question you face. The following six steps provide the basic outline of a process designed to facilitate this listening. The indented questions and directions are simply prompts to help you go further with listening to your body. The questions are intended to be as open-ended as possible, and may feel a bit vague. Feel free to ask other questions. If you need additional guidance or want to learn more, you will find additional resources online (see note 8).

If, at any time, one of these steps feels wrong or jarring to your body, stop following that instruction and reverse the process a bit. Go back to the point where you first noticed your body registering the jarring sensation and stay at that point until you can sense exactly what is happening. Then adjust the process in light of what you have just discovered. In this way, you will eventually develop your own path to listening to your body.

1. Register what is present in your body. Clear a space inside of yourself.

How are you? What's between you and feeling fine? Don't answer this question with language; let what comes in your body do the answering.

Don't go into that sensation. Simply greet it and put it aside for a while, next to you.

Except for that sensation, are you fine? Repeat this question until the major sensations in your body are, figuratively speaking, set out around you.

2. Experience the felt sense.

Pick one problem, situation, or issue present in your life right now to focus on. Don't go into it, though; instead, answer: What do you sense in your body when you recall the whole of that problem, situation, or issue? Sense all of it, the whole thing, the murky discomfort or the unclear body sense of it.

3. Get a handle on it; find words that express the felt sense.

What is the quality of your felt sense? What one word, phrase, or image comes out of this felt sense and describes it best?

4. Resonate, compare, refine.

Go back and forth between word (or image) and your felt sense. Is it an accurate descriptor?

If the word and the sensation match, repeat the sensation of matching several times by going back and forth between the problem, issue, or question and the sensation, each time reexperiencing the felt sense.

If the felt sense changes, follow it with your attention, seeing where it will take you.

When you get a clear match—that is, when the words (images) feel in sync with your body's sensation—let yourself feel that for a minute.

5. Ask questions of the felt-sense.

"What is it, about the whole problem, that makes me so _____?"

If you become stuck, ask other questions: What is the worst of this feeling? What's really so bad about this? What does it need? What should happen? Don't answer; wait for the feeling to stir and give you an answer.

What would it feel like if it was all okay? Let the body answer: What is in the way of that feeling?

6. Receive the wisdom that comes through the felt sense.

Welcome what came to you through your felt sense. Be glad it spoke. It is only one step in exploring your problem, issue, or question, not the last. Now that you know where it is, you can leave it and come back to it later.

Does your body want another round of focusing, or is this a good stopping place?

A FINAL MEDITATION

From the eleventh century, Simeon the New Theologian offers us a stunning meditation on the body. After you reflect on his words, you might find it helpful to return to the chapter's first exercise, Approaching

Discernment through the Body, and see if your body offers you more or different assistance for your discernment. If so, add your new insights to your journal. The body's wisdom is powerful, but subtle. Its wisdom bears deep pondering.

> We awaken in Christ's body
> as Christ awakens our bodies,
> and my poor hand is Christ, He enters
> my foot, and is infinitely me.
>
> I move my hand, and wonderfully
> my hand becomes Christ, becomes all of Him
> (for God is indivisibly
> whole, seamless in His Godhood).
>
> I move my foot, and at once
> He appears like a flash of lightning.
> Do my words seem blasphemous?—Then
> open your heart to Him
>
> and let yourself receive the one
> who is opening to you so deeply.
> For if we genuinely love Him,
> we wake up inside Christ's body
>
> where all our body, all over,
> every most hidden part of it,
> is realized in joy as Him,
> and He makes us, utterly real,
>
> and everything that is hurt, everything
> that seemed to us dark, harsh, shameful,
> maimed, ugly, irreparably
> damaged, is in Him transformed
>
> and recognized as whole, as lovely,
> and radiant in His light
> we awaken as the beloved
> in every last part of our body.[9]

7

Imagination's Insight

Imagination can be a powerful assistance in discernment because, through it, we can try on various scenarios and test out possibilities before we settle on one path. In this chapter, we learn to befriend the imagination, examine the creative possibilities in imagination, and look at how images have been used in the biblical and spiritual traditions. The exercises follow the same trajectory: the first leads us through a simple process for accessing and using the imagination in discernment, the second helps us work deeply with a central image, and the third introduces us to the discernment practices that Ignatius of Loyola used that employ imagination.

If imagination comes easily to you, you will want to include it in your discernment prayer on a regular basis. Imagination, however, needs partners to make sure that it is grounded in reality. Reason can provide just such a complement; we look at this entry point in the next chapter. For now, however, tune up your imagination! If you have prayed with any other entry points, you already have present in your discernment some fodder for your imagination to ponder. If you are beginning here, your imagination can get the creative juices running.

Practice: Approaching Discernment through Imagination

This prayer gives you the opportunity to try on options in your imagination and see what you learn about your proposed decision. If you don't see things in your mind, don't worry. Imagination uses other avenues as well.

---

1. Renew your prayer for spiritual freedom, asking for the desire to follow God however God may call. Ask for the guidance of the Holy Spirit through your imagination.

2. Center your attention by whatever means is useful for you. For example, take deep, rhythmic breaths or repeat a one- or two-word prayer and let it drift off into silence. Rest in the silence for a few moments.

3. Recall the situation or issue you are discerning. If more than one possibility has occurred to you, imagine how each of these alternatives could work out, one at a time. Let your imagination construct scenarios that do not yet exist.

OR

Visualize a possible scenario that could arise from your decision.

4. Now imagine yourself actually choosing what you imagined or visualized. Put yourself into that scene as an active participant. Notice what happens when you do. Write down the outcome.

5. Imagine yourself taking a different path. Write about what that path opens up.

6. Begin to assess the options by answering the following in your journal:

Which course of action flowed most freely?

Which one excited you the most?

Which seemed "right" to you?

Which has the most connection with your personal history?

7. As you imagine yourself following this freer, more right, and more integrated path, how does the option feel to you? What have you learned about your tentative decision? Offer this learning and your tentative decision back to God.

BEFRIENDING THE IMAGINATION

"I don't have any imagination, so I can't do this exercise." How often I hear that! It is surprising how many people believe they do not have any imagination. I used to think it of myself, having internalized this judgment somewhere in my grade-school education. I was happily relieved of my self-limiting judgment during a guided retreat many years ago. My retreat guide listened as I recounted what happened during my time of prayer over the resurrection appearance of Jesus to Mary Magdalene. He noticed that I was outside the scene looking in and suggested that I actually go into the scene with my imagination. As I entered the scene, the garden melted into a seashore, and I recognized the vaguely familiar figure who had just said, "Elizabeth!" I ran to him and gave him a huge hug! Needless to say the text's impact on me after I entered it with my imagination was far greater than when I pondered it from outside. That experience taught me the power of my imagination and freed me to use it in prayer, a gift for which I shall be eternally grateful. I began to reexamine my judgment that "I have no imagination," to deconstruct it and to learn to say of myself, "Indeed I do have a great deal of imagination of various kinds."

If you have made a similar judgment about yourself, you might want to try some simple experiments:

—Mentally select the clothes you will wear tomorrow. With those clothes, what shoes will you wear?

—You smell frying bacon (or some other smell with happy associations). Where does your imagination take you?

—Where does your mind go when you are doing some repetitive task like mowing the lawn or washing the dishes?

—If you had a favorite place as a child, go there now in your imagination.

—Say or think, "When I was a kid, we . . . ," and tell a story that comes to mind.

—Beginning with "It was a dark and stormy night" (or "Once upon a time long ago"), create a story.

In all these cases, your imagination is at work. Part of the problem may be that we often imagine that imagination means only visualizing something in our minds, but not everyone's imagination is strongly visual. In fact, there are many kinds of imagination. The author who sees the end of the story before it is written, the composer who hears the melody and chords in his head, the gardener who uses the winter months to create the plan of next year's garden, the athlete who spends the few minutes before the match mentally reviewing every move she will make, the dancer who warms up so his muscles will be able to execute long-practiced moves, the Scripture scholar who painstakingly re-creates the social location of the particular biblical text prior to working out her interpretation, a parent who tries to understand why her infant is crying, a person who tries to grasp his friend's pain—all these people are employing imagination to create a bridge from what is to what might be: a story with a complicated twist, a jazz riff, a well-planned garden, a skilled athletic performance, a graceful dance, a text understood, an infant cared for, and a friend heard. We all have—and exercise—imagination.

THE CREATIVE IMPULSE OF IMAGINATION

Why might we want to cultivate imagination for use in discernment? If you moved directly from intuition to imagination in your discernment, you may have noticed that intuition and imagination are quite closely related. Yet, though intuition often uses imagination to communicate, imagination is far more than a mouthpiece for intuition. We have more conscious control of our imagination than of our intuition. Imagination's plasticity and potential to facilitate creative breakthroughs make it an invaluable partner for discernment when it is set within a context of faith.[1]

Imagination's great contribution is that it can form images of what is not immediately present, and thereby create visions of new possibilities, the quality on which the first exercise capitalizes. Artistic imagination has given us stunning masterpieces of art, literature, and poetry. Practical imagination (which may sound like an oxymoron) studies situations and sees ahead to improvements or solutions to problems. Through imagination we can project our future and bring into the present the past that is buried in our memory. Imagination can compose, decompose, and recompose the meaning of our life. It can fill dry data or flat experiences with meaning and purpose. It can creatively apply something from one part of life to another, all without committing ourselves to whatever we imagine. Poet Peter Levitt notes, "Imagination is the place in which all boundaries, which are usually determined by the restricted sense of self that our ego promotes, can disappear."[2]

There are other convincing reasons to cultivate imagination for use in discernment. On the scale of cognitive acts, imagination remains nearest the event.[3] Reason draws deductions and creates abstractions. Imagination, in contrast, knows things in their concrete particularity and their accompanying emotions. It is this closeness to the experience, as well as the emotional resonance that accompanies imagination, that makes it so powerful; emotions, after all are what move us to act. Since reason and imagination together help us appropriate and understand an experience in all its fullness, they both have their place in discernment.

A further reason to befriend imagination is that it is so crucial to the spiritual life: the language of knowing God is primarily the language of the imagination. As John Henry Newman noted, belief begins and grows not through a notion or concept, but in the image or symbol. Imagination is thus central to faith and prayer—and discernment.[4]

Once we admit the legitimacy of imagination in our prayer and discernment, we are faced with a two-pronged issue: how do we know that it is God that we are hearing and not just our own imaginations? Puritan John Bunyan, author of *Pilgrim's Progress* and *Grace Abounding to the Chief of Sinners*, can help answer the first part of this dilemma, for he struggled with a similar question. In his writing, Bunyan relied for much detail on the Bible and grounded his theological perspective in Calvin and Luther, but his story came from his own personal experience. He stitched all these sources together with his imagination to create a religious masterpiece. His Puritan coreligionists, however, were deeply suspicious about using the imagination in spiritual writing; Bunyan's kind of allegorical fiction fell outside the boundaries of reason so cherished by the Puritan reformers. In response, Bunyan identified three reasons for eventually publishing *Pilgrim's Progress*: (1) Puritan writers were allowed to write in dialogue that took some liberties with "literal" truth; (2) Scriptures do not deny the use of figures of speech, metaphors, and similies; and (3) the Scriptures used metaphors and analogies, so why, he asked, could he not do likewise?[5]

Wim Wenders, the German filmmaker, also spoke about religious imagination as he portrayed it in his film *Wings of Desire*, a speculative flight of fancy about angels among humans. He imagined the way angels seek to influence us: "The angel realizes that the goal is not to talk into your ears, but to try to live in your eyes." If our eyes were converted, our hearts would follow: may the eyes of our hearts be enlightened so that we may know the hope to which we have been called (Eph. 1:18).[6]

It matters, though, how we nourish the religious imagination. Social activist Andrew Beath relates the following story:

> During a discussion about nonviolence in the face of passionate emotions, a Native American friend told me a story from her tradition. A grandfather told his granddaughter, "I feel as if I have two wolves fighting in my heart. One is vengeful, angry, and violent. The other

is loving, kind, compassionate." The girl asked him, "Grandfather, which wolf will win the fight in your heart?" He answered: "The one I decide to feed."[7]

We are responsible for choosing the imagination we feed. We must ask ourselves: What images am I intentionally putting into my mind? What messages are bombarding my imaginations (and my children's) without my even intending it? What imaginary scenarios do I play over and over again in my mind?

The second part of the dilemma deserves particular attention: How will I know that my imagination is not just me talking to myself? This dilemma can be particularly acute for persons who are suspicious of images. Here, two assertions from deep in the heart of the Christian tradition are foundational and reassuring: "You shall love the Lord your God with . . . all your mind" (Luke 10:27). If our minds are created to imagine as well as reason, then why would God avoid our imaginations in relating to us? Why wouldn't God sometimes come to us in great power through our imaginations? The second piece of the tradition, however, is equally necessary: "You will know them by their fruits" (Matt. 7:20). We must ask what fruits the image brings. If the fruits, over time, look like the list that Paul offers us in Galatians—love, joy, peace, patience, kindness, generosity, faithfulness, and self-control—we can rest assured that we are hearing God through our imagination.

Imagination does have a shadow side, and can offer us crippling and destructive images of ourselves and others. A negative self-image, constructed from some event long in the past, can dog us for years. The imagination can create unreal fears and magnify real fears to the point of crippling us from acting for our own well-being. Imagination can build on a perceived slight and create negative judgment of others, unrelated to their real persons.[8] The challenge we face is to judge images in terms of whether they give life and help increase our faith, hope, and love. Images that don't meet this test are suspect, and they should be questioned and sometimes simply discarded. Professional help may be necessary to disable the power of particularly disturbing self-images. If such images occur in your life, tread cautiously in using imagination as an entry point in your discernment, and always bail out from the exercises should the images become overwhelming. Also, as with all the entry points for discernment, test any tentative decisions that are made through the imagination with other results of discernment through other avenues.

WORKING WITH A CENTRAL IMAGE

Another potentially helpful way we can employ imagination in the service of discernment is to work extensively with one image for the wisdom it contains about our direction. A core image may arise from the inner wisdom lodged deep within us and offer important pointers to major changes we are being invited to make. Like a raft floating from one shore to another, the image carries the wisdom from the unconscious to the conscious mind. The conscious mind can then ponder the image, unlocking the wisdom.

Elizabeth-Anne Vanek reminds us that the authentic image is real, not a fabrication but "a piece of life" that speaks to us about a particular experience, even a state of being. Images can come to us in a variety of ways, including during ordinary activities. They can surface in our dreams and fantasies, or while we're reading Scripture, listening to music, or watching a sunset, for example. We can invite them in our prayer. An image may be exciting, freighted with various emotions, puzzling, or even repulsive, but it also may very well contain something of significance to our lives. A core image is a creation of each unique person. It contains something already known deep within, a wisdom that cannot come from without.[9] The following exercise may help you welcome and work with core images.

Practice: Image Guidance[10]

This exercise helps prepare you to receive an image from within, and then gives some simple steps to help you unpack its significance. If you already have an image, but want to unfold its significance for your discernment, use steps 1–2 and 6–9. If you are used to working with dreams, dream interpretation processes also work well for unpacking other images; use what is helpful to you.

1. Find a quiet, uncluttered place, a place where prayer comes easily and where you will not be disturbed. Make yourself comfortable. Mentally and emotionally free yourself from immediate demands and from the need to watch the clock.

2. Remind yourself of God's presence. Ask God to speak to you through your image work.

3. Think about how your life has been going in terms of prayer, play, work, relationships. Spend some time sifting through where you are, perhaps reading over journal entries, or remembering significant encounters or recent events. The following questions, and others like them, may guide you in this review:

—Has anything unusual happened to me recently?
—Has anything shifted inside me?
—Have I experienced God calling me to something new at this time?
—Have any unusual gifts and graces come to me lately?
—Have I been restless or dissatisfied?
—Have old issues resurfaced or new ones come to the fore?
—Do I notice any patterns in terms of my attitudes and reactions?
—Is anything upsetting me?
—Is there an aspect of my life that I would like to change?

4. When you are in touch with your own emotional climate, do any images come to mind that reflect what you are feeling? If nothing surfaces, do not force anything.

5. Relax yourself through deep breathing. Let everything go from your surroundings and from inside your mind until it is like a blank screen.

6. Concentrate all your attention on your image, if you have one; think of nothing else. If no image has surfaced, simply wait, quietly, keeping your mind a blank screen until something appears.

7. Become a spectator; watch your image unfold without analyzing it or judging it. Be aware of how you are feeling as it shifts and develops.

8. Feel free to interact with your image. Ask it what it represents and why it has come to you at this time; ask it to reveal its wisdom to you. Listen for its answer. Even if it seems to answer in your own voice, trust the words that come, provided that they call you to life.

9. When you feel that the image has yielded its gift to you, thank it for what you have learned. Spend some time in silent prayer, conscious of your new awareness.

10. Immediately following your prayer, think about what the image experience has meant to you. Record it in your journal.

Here's a simple example from my own life: several years ago, I began to notice some of my as-yet-untenured faculty colleagues struggling with speaking what they felt would be unpopular observations or holding positions that would contradict those of the administration. I kept thinking, *I wish they would speak; we need their wisdom.* I would even tell them that privately, but they continued to hesitate, thinking about their future tenure reviews. About the same time, at a faculty retreat devoted to long-range planning, we were asked to stand in a line in the order of our hiring. I was startled to see that I was only fifth from the head of the line, with almost two dozen strung out behind me. One day as I was praying about the situation of one of my junior colleagues, I realized that I had power that I could use on his behalf. In my inner dialogue with this personal power, I realized that I was a senior faculty person and I should start acting like one. The image of myself as "senior faculty" now comes to me frequently, as I ponder how I should use my influence as a member of the faculty. This image has changed the way I relate to myself, my faculty colleagues, the administration, and the institution itself.

Images come to clarify and reveal. They can help us discern what we are meant to do in a particular situation or how we are meant to be at a particular moment of our lives, as I now ponder my responsibility to the institution and my junior colleagues in my decisions about where to put my energy. Images can help us decide between alternatives. Or they may simply clarify our relationship with God, self, and others. Our attitude toward images must be simultaneously openhanded to receive their communication, but also discriminating about the quality and fruit of any given image, and when we may need to take time out from working with it.[11]

IMAGES IN THE TRADITION

Humankind is created in the image of God. This mystery underlies the belief that our imagination—that is, our ability to construct and work with images—is also beloved of God as part of God's human creation. And imagine we do!

Remember all those wonderful stories from the Old Testament and how they come alive, especially in young imaginations: Cain and Abel, Abraham's call, Joseph being sold into Egypt and then saving his starving family. Remember Moses' survival in among the weeds and Moses' own mother being called to wet-nurse her own baby (clever midwives!). Remember the plagues, the parting of the sea, the cloud by day and the fire by night, and the daily fall of manna. Solomon's judgment caught my attention as a young person (would I ever be so clever to find the real mother?), and so did Elijah's challenge to the prophets of Baal (that little puff of cloud came in the nick of time!). Esther and Judith and Ruth and Naomi: these women have captured the imagination of artists and poets. While the Scriptures may not speak much about imagination, they certainly employ imagination to communicate God's word to us.

Every time Jesus told a parable, he relied on the imagination of his hearers to get the situation, to construct a meaning for the parable. Without imagination, they wouldn't have been able to conjure up a picture of sheep, and the parable of the shepherd who goes looking for a lamb that has strayed is virtually meaningless. Without imagination, Jesus' words in John 10:9, "I am the gate. Whoever enters by me will be saved, and will come in and go out and find pasture," are simply nonsensical. In fact, when we bring Scripture from its original setting to the present, we are employing a tremendous act of the imagination. Every time the Scripture is opened to us, personally or communally, God is making use of our imaginations to continue the process of revelation in the present.

Use your imaginations as we jump to the book of Revelation, which is itself a tour de force of imagination. Listen to this passage:

> Then I saw a new heaven and a new earth. . . . And I saw the holy city, the new Jerusalem, coming down out of heaven from God, prepared as a bride adorned for her husband. And I heard a loud voice from the throne saying,
>
> > "See, the home of God is among mortals.
> > He will dwell with them;
> > they will be his peoples . . . ;
> > he will wipe every tear from their eyes.
> > Death will be no more;
> > mourning and crying and pain will be no more. . . ."
>
> And the one who was seated on the throne said, "See, I am making all things new."
>
> (Rev. 21:1–5)

Imagine this new heaven and earth. Imagine the whole of creation being made new! The author continues to feed our imaginations: this new Jerusalem has towering walls of diamond, streets of gold, gates of pearl, and a foundation of precious stones. Arising from the throne of God and of the Lamb, directly in the center of the city, flows the river of life, and on either side of its banks grows the tree of life with a new kind of fruit each month and leaves for the healing of nations (Rev. 21:11; 22:1–2). What a city this is! How it tugs at our imaginations and resonates with our longings for something far beyond our present reality.[12]

In the long tradition of Christian spirituality, many understood the use of imagination in spiritual writing. We've already seen how John Bunyan explained his use of imagination. Let's turn now to Ignatius of Loyola, who lived about a century prior to Bunyan and who was a major influence on Christian understanding and acceptance of imagination in spiritual formation. In fact, Loyola's conversion was an event of imagination. Confined to bed in his brother's home as he convalesced from a shattered leg, Ignatius asked for books to fill the long days. He was hoping for the tales of knights and ladies to which he was accustomed, but the only books in the household were a *Life of Christ* and *Lives of the Saints*. When his boredom became sufficiently acute, he picked them up. Given to daydreaming about great feats of chivalry, he began to daydream about Christ and the saints. Little by little he noticed the difference in the quality of the two kinds of daydreams: the stories of chivalry left him dry and dissatisfied while imagining the lives of the saints and how he could become a saint not only consoled him in the moment, but even after some time passed left him satisfied and joyful. His evolving imagination was changing his heart.[13]

Not surprisingly, imagination figures prominently in Ignatian prayer. Using imagination to enter actively into biblical texts (the same process my retreat guide suggested I use to enter into the resurrection appearance of Jesus to Mary Magdalene) became central to his *Spiritual Exercises*. Ignatius also made use of imagination in discerned decision making, and he has had great impact on the discernment tradition. Our final imagination exercise is taken from the directions contained in *Spiritual Exercises* for making a choice.[14] In it, he has us imagine three different scenarios—using our imaginations to put ourselves into these situations—and then reflect on what, from that perspective, we will have wanted to choose; then, he says, choose that. Each of these scenarios gives a unique vantage point with which to view the decision you are discerning.

Practice: Three Imaginative Scenarios

1. Clarify the matter about which you are discerning. Bring it to mind as clearly and sharply as you can.

2. Remind yourself that the goal of life is the praise, reverence, and service of God. Ask God, as always, for the grace to desire what God desires on your behalf.

3. Ask God to speak through your imagination about what is the better option to choose.

4. Then, without rushing, consider each of the following scenarios in your imagination. Elaborate on them in writing, if you wish:

   —Imagine that you are a trusted advisor to another person who comes to you for advice about the decision facing you. Wanting the best for that person, what would you encourage that person to do?
   —Imagine yourself at the end of your life, looking back on it. From that vantage point, which path would you have wanted to take?
   —Imagine yourself at the Last Judgment. From that vantage point, how do you wish you have decided?

5. What do these imaginative scenarios say about the decision before you? Perhaps you are ready to make a tentative decision; perhaps you have simply received more data for your discernment process.

6. Conclude with a prayer of gratitude to God for the working of your imagination.

Each of these three imaginative scenarios can help highlight what is more pleasing to God, and thus, from a spiritual point of view, more conducive to your long-term and deep contentment and joy—two words Ignatius explicitly uses in describing these imaginative possibilities.

Imagination is a versatile tool to bring to discernment. You can imagine plausible outcomes, try them on in your imagination, and see how you respond. You can work with core images that point out, in their own way, the direction you seek. You can work with Ignatius's classic imagination exercises. Your own imagination is the only limit on how you might construct your own imaginative discernment exercises.

8

Reason's Considerations

For many people, making a decision means reasoning out the alternatives and picking the most logical one. Indeed, reasoning is an important entry point into discernment, but not the only privileged one, as we have seen. Ignatius of Loyola stressed three: imagination, feelings, and reason. In this chapter, we will discover the strengths and limits of reason and trace the use of reason in Scripture and the spiritual tradition, including one figure from the seventeenth century, Thomas Traherne, and one from the eighteenth, Jonathan Edwards. Our first exercise introduces us to Ignatius of Loyola's method for using reason in decision making. Our second exercise invites us to return to an earlier part of the discernment process, gathering the appropriate data, and updating it. If you have already prayed with several entry points, you may have discovered new facets of your issue—or even an entirely new issue—and may need to gather further data. One important point: this exercise is movable; at any point in your discernment, it may be appropriate to continue your data gathering. I have placed it here because data gathering often stresses the use of reason.

Practice: Approaching Discernment through Reason

This exercise works best with a tightly formed question, so if you have not posed your decision in that form, step 2 will direct you to try to do that. The process of writing pros and cons sometimes brings new things

---

to light, and step 4 offers a pause to note anything new that occurs to you. The crucial verb in this prayer is "weigh" (not "count"). In God's presence, weigh what you have written in each list and, at the conclusion, frame a tentative decision.

1. Prepare yourself to be in the presence of God. Renew your desire to follow God's call once it becomes clear to you.

2. If you haven't already done so, try to frame your discernment issue in the form of a simple question that can eventually be answered by yes or no.

3. Make two columns in your journal or on a piece of paper; label one "pro," the other "con." List in the pro column as many reasons as come to mind for your potential decision. In the con column, list reasons against proceeding in that direction.

4. Reflect on each list in turn, beginning with the cons. As you think of other pros or cons, add them to their respective lists.

5. Notice how the issue appears in light of your reflection. Write about what you notice.

6. Weigh the lists carefully, looking for significance over sheer numbers. In light of this weighing, frame a tentative decision.

7. Renew your desire to follow God's call. Now hold your tentative decision together with your desire to follow God's call. Notice what happens. Record it in your journal.

SEEKING GOD WITH ONE'S MIND

There is no one right way to enter into discernment. Western culture prizes rational processes to such an extent that many people equate knowing with the results of reasoning and ignore or downplay other kinds of knowing, such as through the body, intuition, imagination, and feelings. Each way of knowing offers different data to bring to discernment. Similarly, each process reveals some aspects of the issue you are pondering and obscures other aspects. Because you've already prayed about your issue using at least some of these ways, you've likely noticed these differences. This variety continues as we use rational processes in discernment.

To use this process effectively you must have clearly defined your issue. You may now find the need to return to your original issue and reframe it into a simple declarative sentence. It is also sometimes helpful to break up a particularly complex issue into several smaller parts, each with its clearly defined statement or question. As I've said, the issues for discernment do not always condense into a simple declarative sentence. Sometimes it is necessary to, for example, let your intuition, body, or imagination open up a variety of possibilities before settling on one to work with using the rational process above.

Notice, too, that the key word in the sixth step is "weigh"; it means more than simply counting up the number of items on each list. The idea is to sense which alternative is *weightier*—that is, more significant, pulling you more to it (or repelling you more), impressing you with its clarity, logic, or rightness. There may be only one piece of data written under the "con" column, for example, but it can be so significant that it outweighs all the things written under "pro."

I first learned this method in a teaching workshop in the early 1970s. Imagine my surprise at its similarity to a process suggested by Ignatius of Loyola more than four hundred years ago. Ignatius's original process is actually more complicated than ours:

> I should consider and reason out how many advantages of benefits accrue [from the choice being pondered], all of them solely for the praise of God and for the salvation of my soul; and on the contrary I should similarly consider the disadvantages and the dangers in having it. Then acting in the same manner in the second part, I should consider the advantages and benefits in not having it, and contrarily the disadvantages and dangers in not having it.[1]

Thus, the single column each of "pros" and "cons" originally was a double process: a statement *for* the option, with pros and cons of that, and a statement *against* the option, with pros and cons of that. "Overkill," you might say, and for relatively straightforward decisions, that is probably accurate. In fact, I always presented this exercise in its simpler form until I myself was enmeshed in a discernment that simply wouldn't clarify. This discernment was time-limited and the moment was fast approaching when I would have to make my decision about accepting a request to take a new position. I had tried many of the practices covered in earlier chapters, as well as some that we discuss later. When I used the rational entry point in its simpler form above, I finished the weighing with neither the pros nor the cons seeming persuasive. With nothing to lose, I decided to try Ignatius's more complex version and prepared a statement for and a statement against, and set out to list pros and cons for each. Surprisingly, the four columns generated different data than the two-column version. What's more, buried in one column I had written, "You will resent it if you don't have any time for writing." When I proceeded to the weighing, this point became very "heavy," so much so that I began to ponder what was going on behind what I had written. (I credit my intuition with offering this bit of wisdom for my rational mind to consider.) Ultimately, further prayer and reflection led me to modify the original question and agree to be available *if* the work could be set up in such a way that I would be able to continue writing.

In the practice above, I suggested reflecting on the "cons" first, the opposite of what Ignatius suggested. Why the switch? Ignatius and his first companions adopted this pro/con practice when they met to decide if they were going to form themselves into a group committed to each other by a vow of obedience. Based on their example, it has become a common method for group discernment in our day. As this process moved from individual discernment to group discernment, the psychology of groups has affected the practice. The communal version offers time in which everyone offers reasons against the proposal followed by time in which they all speak for it. People are often freed to discover if God is calling them to something new when all the obstacles are out in the open right away. Furthermore, if all speak to both the weaknesses and strengths, it is less likely that members of the group will solidify into opposing camps, each lobbying for its perspective.

If you want to adapt Approaching Discernment through Reason for group use, spend a good bit of time on step 1, making very clear that the group is not just making a decision but listening for God's call through the decision. Step 2, a clear statement, is just as crucial as in individual discernment. Be on the lookout as well for issues that have more than one part, because it's possible to be for one part and against another. If you are doing your own discernment, you can easily enough adjust to such a double question, but it will throw a group into hopeless confusion. In steps 3–6, separate out the cons and the pros: have everyone pray about and then share the cons, and then do the same with the pros. After another time of prayer in which all present prayerfully weigh everything that has been said, ask each person to offer his or her judgment about the best way to go. If there is consensus, proceed to the confirmation steps (chap. 11); if not, return to steps 3–6 here, and repeat the sequence until a consensus begins to emerge. Such group discernment takes more time than voting, but the results are owned by everyone.

ACCESSING THE WISDOM OF THE TRADITION

God is truth. That is the theological anchor for using one's reason in discernment. There is a deep connection between how people know God and how they know truth. If we pursue our search for truth far enough, it inevitably leads to God. Paul was not alone in recognizing that God's truth permeates all creation, and as we use our minds to probe creation, we come to understand more of God through the things God has made. But Paul also insisted that our minds are darkened by the effects of sin, and, unable to penetrate the distortion caused by sin, humans no longer clearly recognize truth:

> Ever since the creation of the world [God's] eternal power and divine nature, invisible though they are, have been understood and seen through the things [God] has made. So they are without excuse; for though they knew God, they did not honor [God] as God or give thanks to [God], but they became futile in their thinking, and their senseless minds were darkened.
>
> (Rom. 1:20–21)

There is a remedy to this dilemma, thanks be to God: the person of Jesus, through whom a new light shines in the darkness (2 Cor. 4:6). The Holy Spirit reflects this new light into the hearts of believers and draws them into a community that practices restored relationship with God, which leads to a new perception of truth. Once we link the Christian community with a renewed perception of truth, we realize that discernment, as an act of seeking truth, must be set within that community. Christian discernment is not a private prayer between an isolated individual and God, even though we may proceed in intensely personal ways to discern uniquely personal decisions. It is, rather, an act of judgment that takes place within and relies on the context of the believing community, where we learn together to see truth with the eyes of Christ.[2]

But how are we to be sure we recognize truth when we see it? That dilemma is one of the Fourth Gospel's main preoccupations. In a series of confrontations, Jesus keeps pointing to the reality—the truth—about who he is: "If you continue in my word, you are truly my disciples; and you will know the truth, and the truth will make you free" (John 8:31–32). But the bickering among his disciples goes on. Finally, shortly before his death, Jesus speaks plainly to the disciples: "I am the way, and the truth, and the life" (John 14:6). Knowing Jesus leads to knowing all things in Jesus, to a renewed mind, to life, and to the liberty of the children of God, as Paul puts it.

The Fourth Gospel also links the Holy Spirit, community, and truth. The final confirmation of Jesus' teaching would not come until Jesus' imminent death and resurrection—his glorification—had been completed and worked out in the lives of his disciples. But Jesus makes the promise even before his death:

> I still have many things to say to you, but you cannot bear them now. When the Spirit of truth comes, he will guide you into all the truth; for he will not speak on his own, but will speak whatever he hears, and he will declare to you the things that are to come. He will glorify me, because he will take what is mine and declare it to you.
>
> (John 16:12–14)

The Christian tradition has long considered the relationship of understanding to discernment. Augustine clearly believed that discernment arises out of this new act of knowing that is described so clearly in the Fourth Gospel. For Augustine, all things that have or will or could ever exist in time and space exist eternally in God's knowing of them. As the Father knows and expresses himself in the Word or Son, that knowing simultaneously holds all creatures in the mind of God. Among all creatures, humans are most capable of receiving this divine knowing and willing and offering a response of praise.

What do these Augustinian-based insights mean for discernment? Most importantly, they mean that, as we come to deeply know any creature (through reasoning or any other way of knowing), we know something that God also knows and loves. Discovering even a partial truth about that creature can bring us the joy of hearing a word from God addressed directly to us. We come more and more to know and love the truth of all things. We develop a discerning heart as Christ illumines our mind to discern the reality of creatures—as intended by God—and by drawing out of us a yearning that all creatures come to the fullness of divine communion.[3]

Thomas Traherne, a seventeenth-century theologian, mystic, and poet, sees the role of the mind even more expansively. He believed that it is only by means of our thoughts that we see anything. Contemplation of God, for Traherne, involves the mind more than any other faculty, and he believed that when we think as God thinks, we become like God:

> Thoughts are the Angels which we send abroad,
> To visit all the Parts of Gods Abode.
> Thoughts are the Things wherin we all confess
> The Quintessence of Sin and Holiness
> Is laid. All Wisdom in a Thought doth Shine,
> By Thoughts alone the Soul is made Divine.[4]

Becoming more like God is, however, more than just thinking as God thinks, as momentous as this is. It means coming to rejoice in the God who gifts so freely, to rejoice in the gifts God gives so freely, to become gift for others in turn, and to live the joy of this giving and receiving communion. This joyful, expansive communion brings true discernment; we prize it, partake of it, and extend it outward to others.[5]

Traherne belonged to the movement within the Church of England known as the Latitudinarians, who were so taken by divine beauty that they tended to undervalue the seriousness of evil and suffering. Undervaluing evil cannot be charged to Jonathan Edwards, the eighteenth-century American Puritan best known for his sermon "Sinners in the Hand of an Angry God." A truly modern person, he read the philosophies of Locke and Newton, and he took developments in science very seriously. He also participated in the numerous and controversial revivals that swept through his parish in Northampton. The benefits and excesses of these revivals caused Edwards to examine how to discern their effects on communities and individuals. How might we know, for instance, if the revivals are a work of God? More personally, how might I know if my experience is truly saving? His works on discernment, written out of a deep desire to answer these questions, have become spiritual classics.

For Edwards, discernment meant "observing the manner of the operation of a spirit that is at work among people." He carefully observed the quality and direction of the changes that happened because of the revival, and compared these results with norms derived from Scripture. Proceeding in this fashion, he believed, provides relative safety in judging.[6] Edwards focused on the quality of our "affections" in making this judgment (we consider affectivity in the next chapter). Here it is interesting to see how he understood the relationship of reasoning and affectivity: the warmth of the fervent heart and the light of understanding together mark the action of the Spirit. "If the great things of religion are rightly understood they will affect the heart," he concluded.[7] Edwards's insistence that reason and affect must be held together reinforces the need for similar balance in our discernment; we should use both head and heart as we seek to understand how God is calling and what our response might be.

In *Distinguishing Marks of a Work of the Spirit of God* (1741), Edwards examined whether the Great Awakening was a work of God. On the one hand, he anticipated the objections of others to an event that his own experience had taught him ought not to be written off simply as overblown religious enthusiasm. On the other hand, he was also aware of those within the revival movement who promoted excesses and errors and gave the whole revival a bad name.

Edwards was an extraordinarily precise writer. He used the categories of "reliable and unreliable signs" to explore how much we can rely on understanding: what kind of understanding indicates that God is at work? He defines an "unreliable sign" as follows: "What are not evidences that a work that is wrought amongst a people, is not the work of the Spirit of God." Note the double negative: from an unreliable sign we simply cannot tell if the phenomenon is a work of God; it is *inconclusive* as a sign. In terms of the kind of reasoning we might want to exercise in discernment, Edwards lists one inconclusive sign: that errors in judgment and delusions of Satan can be intermixed. That is, to those who pointed to errors of judgment made by participants in the Great Awakening and concluded "this can't be God's work," Edwards would have said, "Finding errors in judgment within the revival neither proves nor disproves that the revival is saving. God doesn't preserve us from making errors of judgment, nor do errors of judgment prove God is not in the work." Edwards also gives a reliable sign of God's work focused on knowing: the movement operates as a spirit of truth, leading persons to truth, convincing them of those things that are true (1 John 4:6).

In *Religious Affections*, Edwards shifted his attention from revivals to individual conversion experience amid a revival. He wants to make a judgment (discernment) about whether the experience was a true and saving experience of God. One reliable sign reads as follows: "Gracious [i.e., saving] affections arise from the mind being enlightened, rightly and spiritually to understand or apprehend divine things."

> Holy affections are not heat without light; but evermore arise from the information of the understanding, some spiritual instruction that the mind receives, some light or actual knowledge. . . . Truly spiritual and gracious affections . . . arise from the enlightening of the understanding to understand the things that are taught of God and Christ in a new manner. There is a new understanding of the excellent nature of God and His wonderful perfections, some view of Christ in His spiritual excellencies and fullness. Things that appertain to the way of salvation by Christ are opened to him in a new manner and he now understands those divine and spiritual doctrines which once were foolishness to him.[8]

In other words, the fruit of our knowing is the judge of its efficacy. Do we, as a result of knowing, understand God and God's ways more? Do we grasp the heart of Christ more deeply? Do we resonate with a truth of creation that reflects the Creator? Is our mind gradually being more and more conformed to Christ? Edwards says in his context what Paul said in his:

> Those who are unspiritual do not receive the gifts of God's Spirit, for they are foolishness to them, and they are unable to understand them because they are spiritually discerned. Those who are spiritual discern all things, and they are themselves subject to no one else's scrutiny.
>
> "For who has known the mind of the Lord
>   so as to instruct him?"
> But we have the mind of Christ.
>   (1 Cor. 2:14–16)

TAKING A WIDER PERSPECTIVE

The thinking/weighing process appeals to the rational self in all of us. To those who are primarily thinkers by nature, it is the primary decision-making process. The problem is that, although many persons assume it is the only process which counts in decision making, it is as susceptible to blindness as any other mode of decision making. Ignatius suggested his rational method was appropriate when we are not moved by strong feelings of any kind. I would also suggest that this approach be used by persons who are rationally inclined, the so-called thinkers in the Myers-Briggs typology, for example, but always in conjunction with at least one other approach, one that arises from very different ways of approaching reality.

Two further notes: Every entry point can also be used both to reach a tentative decision (which is how I have been presenting them) and to gather data that undergirds and feeds into another entry point for discernment. Logically organizing the information necessary to come to a decision is an important function of reason in service to discernment. One could, for example, identify options by intuition or imagination, and refine them by using reason in gathering further data and weighing pros and cons. Once you grasp the various entry points, you can use them with great flexibility, weaving them in and out of different moments of the larger process in the first chapter that has been guiding us through our discernment:

—Seek the inner disposition of spiritual freedom upon which discernment rests.
—Discover and specify the issue or choice.
—Gather the appropriate data.
—Reflect and pray continuously, but especially throughout the weighing process.
—Using one or more of the entry points, formulate a tentative decision.
—Seek confirmation from God.
—Assess the process and learn from looking back.

With this kind of mutual interaction and reinforcement, our sevenfold way of moving through discernment to a decision becomes more like a graceful dance than a lockstep march.

Second, we see that accurate data is particularly important to the reasoning process. But accurate data supports all the entry points, not just reasoning. Now that you are a ways into your discernment, it might be important to step back for a larger view of your process. Did one entry point suggest something on which you need to follow up? Has your question become more nuanced or changed completely? Do you need more data? Do you need a different kind of data? The next exercise invites you to prayerfully examine these questions. You can use it, as well, to summarize and focus what you have done so far.

Practice: Reviewing and Revisiting Your Discernment

1. Stop! Let silence deepen around you. Remember why you are discerning: you are seeking the path that will give you the deepest satisfaction because you are giving greater glory to God. Spend some time allowing God to call forth in you the desire to hear and follow God's call. Do not be in a hurry to move to the next point.

2. Return to the journal in which you have kept your discernment notes. Review all you have done so far.

3. Has your question shifted as a result of your process? If so, you may need to gather more data for this revised discernment situation. What information do you need to gather in order to make an informed decision? How/when will you gather it? The questions in Gathering Relevant Data in chapter 3 might be helpful here.

4. If your discernment question has not changed significantly, review the data you have gathered for it. What is still missing? When/how will you gather it?

5. As you review the data, think about how it impacts the decision you are considering. What weight do you give it? Does it suggest any particular decision? How do you feel about moving in this direction?

Ignatius closed his reasoning process by directing the discerner to offer the decision to God and allow God to confirm it. We have been following Ignatius's wisdom by insisting on a period of confirmation, and so each of the entry points terminates in a tentative decision. In the final chapter, I provide a process for bringing a tentative decision to God for confirmation. At that point, you will conclude your discernment.

After praying with two or three entry points, you may get a pretty clear sense of where your decision lies. When that point comes is unique to each person and each discernment—it's your decision, you chose how to approach it, and you will know when you feel done. At that point, you have some options. What you should *not* do is simply make the decision and set about implementing it. When you feel ready to complete the discernment, then use the exercises in chapter 11 to confirm your decision and evaluate your process. The time spent on confirmation allows God to let us know that we are on the right track—or not. Of course, you are free to continue praying with other entry points; each additional one gives you an opportunity to deepen your sense of what God is calling you to do. Often these additional entry points begin to take on the feel of confirmation in their own right— your spirit keeps saying yes to your tentative decision.

As careful and precise as Ignatius was in his reasoning process, his preferred entry point was through feelings. To this entry point we now turn.

9

The Power of Religious Affections

With this entry point, we enter the realm of feelings[1] in discernment. Many people have been taught to avoid feelings when making an important decision, but the discernment tradition gives them an important, though qualified, place. We look first at how to befriend our feelings for purposes of discernment, then at the biblical perspective on emotions, Jonathan Edwards on the meaning of religious affections and their impact on discernment, and Ignatius of Loyola on two particular religious affections key to discernment: consolation and desolation. We shall begin, as usual, with an exercise that invites us to bring our feelings into discernment. Since Ignatius used consolation and desolation both to point toward a decision and as part of confirming a decision, we shall follow his lead in the second exercise, where we review our entire process to this point and notice the presence of either consolation or desolation at every step.

Practice: Approaching Discernment through Feelings

What do your feelings tell you about your issue? After noticing the whole range of feelings, this prayer asks you to check for two that are key in discernment. If using your feelings to come to a decision seems risky, remember that other entry points balance the contribution that feelings make to your discernment.

---

1. Allow yourself to become aware of God's presence, God's love and care for you personally. Rest for as long as you wish in the sense of God's love. Renew your desire to follow God's call as it unfolds through your decision.

2. Review all the options you are considering, noting all the feelings they arouse in you. Record the feelings in your journal, taking care not to overlook ones that you don't like or that seem off-base.

3. If you were going to make a decision just on the basis of these feelings, toward what are you inclined? How do you feel about that possibility? Record these feelings as well.

4. Sit with the tentative decision that is forming, along with all its accompanying feelings, to see what it produces in you.
    Does it produce consolation? a sense of increasing faith, hope, love, peace with God, others, and oneself? a rightness that is deeper than just feeling good?

OR

    Do you sense desolation? a lessening of faith, hope, and love? restlessness, discouragement, heaviness, disinclination to proceed, a sense of wrongness? (God may indeed call us despite our fear or hopelessness or other negative feeling; if so, the sense of rightness will be deeper than the sense of discomfort.)

5. Revise your tentative decision based on this sense of consolation or desolation. Note in your journal your tentative decision and the inner movements that led to it.

BEFRIENDING FEELINGS

Approaching Discernment through Feelings invites us to notice our feelings, and then to focus on two, which Ignatius of Loyola named "consolation" and "desolation." But perhaps you don't know how you feel, on the one hand, or are overwhelmed with feelings and can't think straight on the other. Some context for using feelings in discernment may help with both responses.

The language of faith is, in large part, the language of feelings. Spiritual life is the passion for God expressed through our unique selves and our unique contexts. The power of emotion lies in its ability to move us to action. If we don't feel anything, we probably don't act. Consequently, intentionally bringing our feelings into our discernment invites us to consider what empowers us to move forward. For many people, however, bringing feelings to discernment is not easy.

I remember as a young person being warned against trusting my feelings. Depending on who was imparting the warning, the message came in various cautionary words: "You can get swept away by your feelings, and before you know it you've gone too far!" Or, when I couldn't muster enthusiasm for something (like my homework), I was told, "Do it anyhow. It doesn't matter how you feel." In the rough-and-tumble of neighborhood play came the regular "Crying is for sissies." Since I have always had very strong feelings, this kind of advice was never very helpful and taught me to doubt my feelings as trustworthy guides.

Our religious education may also have confounded our relationship to our feelings. Some feelings, we learned, were actually deadly sins: anger, hatred, and envy, for example. On the other hand, love was also bounded by many fences. Some love was encouraged, but other kinds actively discouraged. We may even have internalized the admonition, "If it feels good, it must be bad!" Many parts of the religious tradition have relegated feelings to an inferior, even suspect, status and worked against using feelings as an integral part of discernment. People from this kind of religious upbringing usually have some remedial work to do around feelings before they can fully trust their role in discernment.

Fortunately, there's been a recent move toward a more holistic spirituality that embraces feelings. Theologian and spiritual director Kathleen Fischer offers the following two principles to foster the integration of emotions into our spiritual life: (1) Emotions belong at the center of spirituality, not at its edges. (2) Emotions are not opposed to reason; in fact, they are a form of reason.[2]

It took me a while to accept the idea of the centrality of emotion. I thought for a long time that I could squelch "dangerous" emotions and only encourage "positive" ones. Throwing tantrums as a child got me into trouble, so I learned to batten down my frustration and rage. Jealousy fractured friendships and sometimes forced my friends to choose between me and another, so I learned to tone down expressing my need for attention. It was a struggle for me to learn that all feelings were attached to each other and that I couldn't have the "good" ones if I insisted on denying the "bad" ones. I had to learn to come to terms with my less-than-desirable ones in a different way than by simply "stuffing" them. Fortunately, I discovered that the emotions that caused me trouble could actually be brought before God. As I did that, I eventually became more able to let God's grace work on me, transforming the unruly emotions from the inside out. Rather than deny whole parts of myself, I could turn them over to God, and with God's grace begin to integrate in more positive ways in my life the energy that comes from frustration, anger, and jealousy.

Think of the richness that emotions add to our lives. The awe inspired by a spectacular sunset, the thrill of a massive organ booming out an intricate toccata, the grief upon the loss of a spouse, the gratitude for a moment of silence in the middle of a hectic day, the spontaneous rush of love at seeing a grandchild for the first time, the determination to help that arises when a friend is in trouble—these feelings not only connect us with one another, but also to God. Any aspect of experience can mediate the divine, and in fact, a deep abiding conviction of God's love for us grounds a healthy emotional life. When we are convinced that God loves us exactly as we are, with all of our feelings and rebellions, we can then be about the business of integrating our emotions into a healthy spirituality.[3]

Let's turn to Fischer's second guideline: emotions are themselves a kind of reasoning; they are not in opposition to reasoning—in fact, all reasoning has some level of emotion attached to it. Those who have suffered from severe depression, the extreme flattening out of emotions, know how hard it is to do anything, even get up in the morning, and how difficult it is to follow a thought all the way through to its conclusion. Contrast the passion (an emotion!) of a writer to find the right word, the determination of a day laborer to put food on his family's table, the pride of a young mother as she plays with her infant, the compassion of a nurse's aide as she attends to a bedridden elder. If we divide the word into its constituent parts, e-motion, it is easy to see that it means "toward motion." We cannot make sound decisions without emotions. They constitute an essential component of knowing and judging.

There is a big difference between having feelings and acting on them. We become even more comfortable in admitting emotions into discernment when we recognize that difference. Emotions arise spontaneously as a bodily response to what is happening to us in a given moment. We can learn to differentiate that moment, largely out of our control, from our response, which *is* in our control. With some practice, we can learn to read our emotions. We can learn to ask ourselves: What am I passionate about here? Why is this making me angry? What's this unease about? We can learn that we do have choices about our emotions and that it is possible to fuel some and let others wither. We can begin to ask how God's Spirit might be prompting us to respond to a given feeling. Finally, we can learn to notice the changes in our emotions over time and ask what that shift might mean. All these ways of working with our emotions contribute greatly to the process of discernment.

BIBLICAL AND TRADITIONAL PERSPECTIVES

Feelings permeate the Scriptures. Vivid characters express strong emotions. Think of Cain's jealousy at Abel's virtue, Sarah's skepticism at the visitors' prophecy, Rachel's envy at Leah's fertility, Jacob's grief at the loss of Joseph, or David's remorse when Nathan confronted him with his sin. Remember Ruth's attachment to her mother-in-law Naomi, Esther's courage in fighting for her people, and Jonathan and David's great mutual affection: "When David had finished speaking to Saul, the soul of Jonathan was bound to the soul of David, and Jonathan loved him as his own soul" (1 Sam. 18:1).

The magi were overwhelmed with joy at seeing the child Jesus, but a few miles away, Herod was infuriated that they had tricked him. Simeon and Anna spontaneously broke into praise of God when they saw Jesus. Mary, for her part, "treasured all these things in her heart." And remember Jesus' strong emotions—his grief and tears at Lazarus's tomb, his anger and prophetic action in overturning the money-changing tables, and his own anguish the night before his death when its inevitability stared him fully in the face. John's Gospel speaks of "the disciple whom Jesus loved," so the feelings Jesus had for this disciple could be observed by others. Remember Peter, overwhelmed by fear, denying Jesus and then weeping bitterly at what he had done. Peter and Paul had serious disagreements, and Paul "opposed him to his face" (Gal. 2:11). Nor was Paul shy about scolding his churches when they alarmed or disappointed him.

But it is the psalms that really tutor our religious affections, for in them we find every human emotion laid right out in front of God. In the psalms, intense emotions are turned into prayer. Praying the psalms can help us get in touch with emotions that we would rather not admit to ourselves, let alone to God.

Psalm 137 is a worst-case example. It begins with the grief and longing of the people from the land of exile:

By the rivers of Babylon—
> there we sat down and there we wept
> when we remembered Zion.
On the willows there
> we hung up our harps.
>   (Ps. 137:1–2)

But in that grief and longing, the psalmist also levels a horrible curse on the captors:

Happy shall they be who pay you back
> what you have done to us!
Happy shall they be who take your little ones
> and dash them against the rock!
>   (Ps. 137:8–9)

Judging inappropriate the curse leveled at the captors' children, liturgists routinely excise at least this part, and often the whole psalm, from public worship. I believe, though, that censoring emotions like rage from our worship actually sells the congregation short. It leaves them with the impression that only "positive" feelings are worthy of prayer—a message akin to my childhood warnings against feelings that I internalized. Educators have a name for the teaching that occurs when something is never mentioned; they call it the "null curriculum." The null curriculum in our churches too often teaches that if we have rage, anger, or other strong emotion, then we don't belong in church.

What Psalm 137 does, though, is actually far more radical than simply naming the rage the captives felt. The psalmist puts all those feelings right out there before God, and gives over to God the responsibility for making things right, for bringing justice: "Remember, O LORD . . ." From this psalm we learn that not only can we have such powerful emotions, we can bring them to God—and we can attend to them as part of our discernment.

Two ancient spiritual writers, Origen and Athanasius, help us move from accepting our feelings and bringing them into our prayer to using them as part of discernment. Origen (185–254) was one of the earliest Christian thinkers to comment systematically on the role of affections in discernment. He taught that when passions and emotions run so high that they cloud personal freedom, a spirit other than the Holy Spirit is at play. So, if we feel compelled to act or think in certain ways, we should be suspicious that we lack the freedom that grounds discernment. On the other hand, if our inner liberty is preserved and grows, it is a sign that the Holy Spirit is at work.[4] Discernment, we learn from Origen, should always lead to greater spiritual freedom.

In his *Life of Antony*, Athanasius (c. 357) also takes up a discussion of positive or negative signs that the Holy Spirit is at work. Athanasius held that when feelings are either very strong or widely vacillating— enough to perturb a person's calm—we should be suspicious that the Holy Spirit is not behind it. Confusion and din cause fear, dejection, grief, remorse, and the like. The presence of the Holy, by contrast, "comes so quietly and gently that immediately joy, gladness, and courage arise in the soul." Fear is taken away and replaced by strength, calmness of thought, joy, and a settled state.[5] Eleven hundred years later, Ignatius of Loyola offered a striking metaphor to capture this distinction: "In the case of those going from good to better, the good angel touches the soul gently, lightly, and sweetly, like a drop of water going into a sponge. The evil spirit touches it sharply, with noise and disturbance, like a drop of water falling onto a stone."[6] Ignatius also systematized the notions of consolation and desolation; their description will await the treatment of one further concept, religious affections.

RELIGIOUS AFFECTIONS

So far we have spoken of feelings and emotions, using these two words interchangeably. But there are two related terms in the discernment tradition, "affections" and "affectivity." Affectivity is the ability to feel emotions and respond to them, the capacity to be touched by and respond to someone or something.[7] In the eighteenth century, the great American theologian Jonathan Edwards introduced this terminology in his important works related to discernment. "True religion, in great part, consists in holy affections," he says.[8] For Edwards, affections are more than emotions or mental preferences; rather, they involve a coordinated interplay of thinking, feeling, and acting—a coordinated interplay of mind, will, and feelings.[9] Edwards also realized that it is possible to make choices about our affections: "A man's having much affection does not prove that he has any true religion, but if he has not affection, it proves that he has no true religion. The right way is not to reject all affections nor to approve all; but to distinguish between affections, approving some and rejecting others."[10]

Think of affections as a complex interrelationship of thought, feeling, and willing that allows us to respond in one way rather than another. Christian affections are this complex interrelationship set within the context of our desire to follow Christ, our patterns of prayer, and our habitual ethical responses. Contrition is a good example of a Christian religious affection. It is more than feeling bad, guilty, or even remorseful, though it may be touched by any or all of these feelings. It is a deep recognition of who God is and how I have offended God (thoughts), sorrow for this breach of relationship (feeling) and a clear commitment to changing one's behavior in the future (choice).

Two significant religious affections in discernment are consolation and desolation. Both are frequently misunderstood. Consolation does not mean feeling good, nor does desolation mean feeling bad. Since these two religious affections play a central role in classical Christian discernment, it is important to be clear what they mean and how to use them.

For Ignatius of Loyola, consolation comprises three things: (1) feelings such as peace and gladness (also "negative" feelings such as remorse, if they draw us toward God); (2) the causes of such feelings (ultimately the Holy Spirit); and (3) the positive consequences of these particular feelings (such as greater hope, faith, and charity). Desolation is exactly the opposite and contains: (1) feelings such as darkness, turmoil, discouragement, unhappiness, and tepidity; (2) the cause of such feelings (ultimately a spirit opposed to the Holy Spirit); and (3) the results of such feelings, namely, a decrease in hope, faith, and love.[11]

Why does it matter that we understand consolation and desolation? Because once we recognize spiritual desolations, the affective obstacles to our spiritual life, we can resist and even reject them. They create a slippery slope that leads us away from where we want to go, which is, of course, closer to God. On the other hand, we can delight in spiritual consolations, using the encouragement that they give to strengthen our spiritual walk. We can also store up memories of the encouragement for the times that will surely come when we have a tougher time staying the course.[12]

Ignatius's use of consolation and desolation was rooted in an underlying faith that the reliable sign of the Holy Spirit's work is an increase of faith, hope, and love. He believed that we can sort out our feelings by that touchstone; if they foster an increase of faith, hope, and love, we are discerning aright. But if you find yourself with less faith, hope, or love, be suspect that the path you are on is not the best way to follow God.

It is not enough simply to identify the particular feelings and follow the ones that feel good. A more nuanced judgment is necessary, based on what happens to our faith, hope, and love. For example, suppose someone experiences a wonderful sense of delight and expectation, but if his delight comes because he has just sold silver he stole from his mother's home to buy his evening's drugs, then clearly this feeling does not increase faith, hope, and love. On the other hand, if a preschool teacher experiences delight and expectation as she sees her little charges lining up to sing for their parents, her feelings probably do lead to greater love for these children and their families, and increase her commitment to her hard and often-thankless work on behalf of the children. In the first case, the feelings, though pleasant, fall into the category of desolation, but in the second case, the feelings are clearly a consolation.

Of course, Ignatius would understand that interior freedom from compulsion, the humble desire for God, consolation of a sense of mission, and greater attunement to Christ acting in the persons and world would be other ways that faith, hope, and love are manifested. He would probably add his resounding yes to Jonathan Edwards's signs of gracious (i.e., saving) affections, including a new spiritual perception and hunger for God, increased wisdom, humility, gentleness, conviction and certitude, greater balance, an open mind and a softened heart, and, of course, actual fruit in Christian practice. The term "consolation" summarizes many manifestations of the Holy Spirit.

In Approaching Discernment through Feelings, I cautioned that sometimes God is calling despite your "negative" feelings. Suppose you've fallen into the habit of staying in bed on Sundays because you enjoy feeling lazy. A little prick of regret could be the Holy Spirit nudging you to renew your connection to the faith community. Suppose, as you approach a momentous decision that you know will cause resistance in others, you feel anxious or afraid. Does that mean God is not calling you to that decision? Not necessarily. Follow the faith, hope, and love as you sort through the feelings. Does your proposed action flow from your deep integrity? Does it lead you to greater faith that God will be with you? Will significant good come from it? Then probably God is calling you to it despite the presence of anxiety and fear. You can look for a deep sense of rightness to carry you through these feelings. Clearly consolation is not just about feeling good, nor desolation about feeling bad.

We return to these authentic signs of the work of the Holy Spirit in our lives when we consider the final step in our discernment process, confirmation. We shall see that consolation will play a key role in our decision to finalize our tentative decision.

LOOKING AT THE WHOLE DISCERNMENT PROCESS

Many people shy away from using feelings in discernment because they know that feelings are fleeting and fickle. They wonder how we can rely on feelings in our discernment when what we feel today may be different tomorrow. Ignatius grappled with this problem and offers us some help. We should, he says, pay attention to the whole course of the discernment, the whole course of our thoughts, the whole course of our feelings. We may start well, with great enthusiasm, but notice over time that our energy was diverted and gradually eroded into nothing. We may have a fine goal, but the means slipped into some questionable areas. The peace we felt as we first pondered a decision gave way to a nagging sense of disquiet after some time, a feeling that had been submerged under the more pleasant feeling of relief in making a decision. If the beginning, middle, and end are all good *and* serve to draw us deeper into faith, hope, and love, we can be confident in our decision.[13] In effect, we are to take one step back from the ebb and flow of feelings and look at the larger picture, in which feelings hold an integral place.

The following practice is based on this Ignatian insight. Because it forms a bridge to the final task of discernment—confirmation—it should be placed toward the latter part of your discernment, when most of your processing has occurred. If you are just beginning your discernment, put this exercise off until just before you bring your tentative decision to God for confirmation.

Practice: The Beginning, Middle, and End

1. In discernment, we seek God's leading for our lives. Begin by renewing your desire to be led by this gracious spirit of God.

2. The first fruit of the Holy Spirit in discernment is a sense of indifference, that is, the desire to let go of anything that might distract from hearing and following God's call. Ask for this grace now.

3. Look back at your discernment process so far. Recall the begin-

---

ning. What desires motivated you to begin? What were you seeking? What feelings surfaced? Were they generally consoling, or were they somehow disquieting? Did they make it harder or easier to continue?

4. Recall the middle part of your discernment. What thoughts, feelings, and motivations characterized this part? If you uncover any lack of clarity, what feelings surfaced in its midst? Did they help you to continue despite the uncertainty, or did they weigh down your spirit? What was the balance between consoling and desolating feelings?

5. As you approach the conclusion of your discernment, what feelings now surface? Again, judge them against the qualities of consolation and desolation.

6. Offer to God what you discover.

With the wisdom of such careful discerners as Ignatius and Edwards, we can affirm the role of feelings in discernment. As with other entry points, we must approach feelings with care, giving them neither too much power nor too little. When we understand them as an integral part of human decision making, we can admit feelings into their proper place in our discernment. This is good news for persons who, like me, are "Feelers" in Myers-Briggs terms and whose primary way of approaching a decision is that ultimately it "feels right." But using feelings in discernment is also good news for those who are inclined to disregard feelings. You too should consider feelings as a part of your discernment; doing so will help you make a more careful and considered decision, while at the same time help you to integrate feelings more consistently into your ways of dealing with the world.

10

Nature's Perspective

All the entry points we have so far explored have directed your attention inside yourself, to your memory, intuition, body, imagination, thoughts, and feelings. This final entry point asks you to go outside into nature. This change of perspective can offer a new angle on your question because you are asking it in the presence of another creature. You are acting on the reality that you are not the center of the universe, but a fellow low creature of the same Creator. This chapter gives a rationale for this move, helps you feel comfortable using nature in your prayer, and constructs a biblical and theological understanding of nature upon which to base discernment. The first exercise, Approaching Discernment through Nature, provides the nature-based discernment practice. The second exercise focuses on receiving nature's revelation; if nature-based prayer is new to you, this prayer can deepen your comfort with it.

Practice: Approaching Discernment through Nature

This exercise is ideally done outdoors. However, if that is not possible or practical, use any natural object, such as a stone, shell, leaf, flower, potted plant, or piece of driftwood as your companion in this prayer. If you choose a deserted place or go out at night, be sure to take care for your safety.

---

1. Go outside. Walk or sit in a place where you feel comfortable.

2. Seek, once again, the inner freedom to desire what God desires and follow it once it becomes clear.

3. As you walk or sit, notice your surroundings. Let your attention be drawn to something natural in the environment, living or non-living. Be present to it as completely as you can. Allow it to be just what it is without trying to change it or use it for your purposes.

4. In the presence of that natural object, restate the decision you are discerning, without describing it in detail or rehearsing its aspects. Simply let your discernment question be present alongside you as you ponder this natural object.

5. Wait, in the presence of this bit of nature, listening for what it might share with you. Note it in detail in your journal.

6. What does your experience of being present to the natural object suggest about your decision?

7. Bring any new awareness about your decision back to your desire to follow God's call. Notice what happens to your thoughts and feelings. Perhaps an image comes to you. Does your decision feel different from this perspective? Record in your journal any shifts.

8. Offer your tentative decision to God.

SHOULD A CHRISTIAN LOVE NATURE?

Some years ago, I read a short essay by theologian Sallie McFague entitled "Should a Christian Love Nature?"[1] It seems like a simple and straightforward question, easy to answer in the affirmative. But surprisingly, many Christians over our long history have not loved nature, and many still don't. Christianity's ambivalence about nature and its place in the spiritual life is not surprising, once one looks at the history of Christian thought.

H. Paul Santmire, ecological theologian and Lutheran pastor, has chronicled this ambiguous history, noting two major paths that Christian thought has taken with respect to nature. In one view, the human spirit rises above nature; in the other, the human spirit is seen as embedded in nature. The first view has been less hospitable to nature than the second, which sees humans' self-consciously embodied selves celebrating God's presence, in, with, and under the whole biophysical order.[2] With the rise of ecological consciousness, other theologians are taking up these issues. Mark I. Wallace, who teaches religion at Swarthmore College, is attempting to reclaim the biblical tradition of the Creator Spirit, the third person of the Trinity, as a way to help heal the breach between Christians and nature.[3] Beatrice Bruteau, mathematician, philosopher, and contemplative, works from the other direction. She begins with contemporary theories of the origin of the universe, the chemistry involved in life, the necessity of evolution, and the neurobiology involved in consciousness and reflects on the notions of incarnation and Trinity.[4] These scholars, among others, indicate that the Christian tradition about humans and God is richer than we often imagine.

McFague wants to answer her own question with a resounding "Yes!" Yes, because "quite simply, God is with us here in and on our earth. That is what the incarnation claims. . . . Physical reality, earthly reality is the place where we find the presence of God—that is what an Incarnational theology tells us."[5] Theologian Mark Wallace extends this incarnational perspective, pointing out that the Holy Spirit dwells at the heart of all living things as its life force: "The *then and there* incarnation of God in Jesus is recapitulated in the *here and now* embodiment of the Spirit in the world—an embodiment that harks back to the originary Parent God's birthing of order out of chaos."[6] All persons of the Trinity, then, are intimately involved with Creation.

Despite such contemporary theological thinking honoring the place of nature in Christian theology—and by extension, Christian life—residues of a long-standing distrust of nature often lie deep in Christian bones. Christians may understand and uphold the notion of stewardship of nature, but *love* nature? That notion is a stretch for many, though sometimes an unconscious one. Subtle dis-ease can sometimes be traced to a notion of nature absorbed from reading Old Testament texts that imply that nature is the place of pagan Baal worshipers. Sometimes it is evoked by contemporary goddess worship or by Wiccan practices. Without even realizing it, good Christians may transfer their unconscious dis-ease about paganism into their approach to nature and avoid seeking God in and through nature. Ironically, in trying to honor their Christian upbringing, they deny God's power to reveal through and in nature.

McFague's question implies a second one: why should a Christian love nature? Those who spend time being contemplatively present to nature give us a clue. Nature is a privileged way to move away from a focus of oneself as the horizon of existence and to the very horizon of ultimate mystery. Nature helps adjust our perspective, moving it from ours toward God's. We begin to see ourselves not as the center of the universe, but as one small part of a vast and interconnected web that is God's creation. Nature invites us to a new and freeing humility.

McFague, however, is at least as much interested in how a Christian should love nature. Here, she follows a simple logic: you cannot love what you do not know. Therefore, if we are to love nature, we must set out to know nature on its own terms—not for what it can do for us. Once we love it, we can trust it to aid us in our quest for God's call in our lives. We do not need grand mountain vistas or sweeping ocean views. Any small portion of nature, any "body," will do. We pay attention, listen to, learn about, and honor this bit of creation in its uniqueness, particularity, and otherness. We come alongside it as one creature to another.[7] This rationale undergirds Approaching Discernment through Nature.

Meister Eckhart reminds us: "If I spent enough time with the tiniest creature—even a caterpillar—I would never have to prepare a sermon. So full of God is every creature."[8] Some of us, however, may need permission and practice in order to become comfortable seeking God in and through nature. Contemporary poet Mary Oliver can tutor us.

Praying

It doesn't have to be
the blue iris, it could be
weeds in a vacant lot, or a few
small stones; just
pay attention, then patch

a few words together and don't try
to make them elaborate, this isn't
a contest but the doorway

into thanks, and a silence in which
another voice may speak.[9]

Once we become accustomed to really seeing what is there, to really knowing it for its own sake, allowing ourselves to be grateful for even a small blade of grass, then we can begin to ask what of God it can reveal to us.

You can use the next exercise in two ways. It can help you deepen your comfort level in seeking God in and through nature, and it can provide some additional suggestions with which to expand step 3 in the first exercise, which simply directs you to be present to your object as to another creature.

Practice: Nature's Revelation[10]

This prayer invites you to use your imagination to enter into dialogue with a natural object. Instead of simply picking any object at hand, you might try letting a natural object pick you.

Choose an object such as a stone, leaf, blade of grass, stick, or other "outside" object.

Sit quietly with your object.

Ask the object about itself, its story, its history.
Where it has been . . .
Who has touched it, held it, walked past it without noticing?
Where was it born? How did it get there?
Sit quietly and wait for answers.

Then ask the object about its inner life, its spirituality.
About its vulnerability, its tenderness, its density, its relations with others.
Sit quietly and wait for answers.

What does it wish to tell you?
What does the object say about your intuitions? your depths?

Finally, what, if anything, does the object tell you of God?

With a practice such as this—and others that you might think of—we can ready ourselves to receive nature's contribution to our discernment. The thesis is simple: God is revealing Godself at every moment through creation. Discernment has a different quality when we intentionally recognize and assume our place in this widest of our contexts, the natural world, of which we are minute specks.

The danger exists, however, for the kind of pragmatism that Sallie McFague warned about to assert itself: using nature to do something for us—in this case, providing a revelation about God. When we come to nature for what it can do for us, even revealing God, we fail to honor nature in its uniqueness. Paradoxically, the result of honoring nature as other, intrinsically valuable in its own right, is that we also learn things we do not easily learn otherwise about ourselves and God. Philosopher Simone Weil (1909–1943) observed that the prerequisite to a reawakened sensitivity to divine presence is to see the world as filled with an unfathomable artistry. As we gradually forgo consuming and possessing the world, its peculiar beauty begins to grow luminous, because the very nature of beauty is that it cannot be consumed. Nature is most vibrant, most evocative, and most resonant when, in its uncommodified beauty, it points beyond itself.[11]

WHAT EXACTLY IS NATURE?

Although I have been speaking as if there exists a common understanding of nature, trying to define the word is notoriously difficult. Nature is not an artifact of a distant God. It is not an indifferent resource at our disposal. It is not a stage upon which history and human experiences are played out. All of these perspectives have held sway in certain eras or under certain theological systems. Nature is that out of which all life arises, including human life. Nature is a fragile, interconnected web of ecological integrity on which all life depends. Given nature's power and fragility, humility is an appropriate posture with which to engage nature.[12]

Part of the enduring confusion about the word "nature" is that it is used to mean either the entire natural world with humans included or the nonhuman natural world with humans over against (usually "above") nature. There is a clear biblical warrant all the way back to Genesis for seeing humans as truly a part of nature, as we shall see. This sense of nature as an interdependent relationship of all material things is what the contemporary science-theology dialogue and ecological theology encourage us to adopt.[13]

The Nicene Creed refers to nature as "all things visible and invisible." This definition, held by Thomas Aquinas, includes in nature every

spiritual entity as well as all material entities. But this inclusive meaning goes beyond our commonsense notion of nature. A more useful
perspective comes from Genesis 1:1, "God created the heavens and the
earth." Nature, or its biblical synonym, "the earth," includes everything
studied in our modern sciences of physics, chemistry, geology, astron-
omy, biology, ecology, and cosmology. Santmire summarizes this biblical position on "the earth" or "nature" as "that realm created, sustained
and consummated by God, and constituted by creatures such as the
stars, the land, the waters, vegetation, the swarms of living things; and
human beings insofar as they are bodily creatures, along with the material and vital products of human creativity, such as gardens or build-
ings."[14] Nature, then, constitutes all material and vital reality, the
"earth" of the creation story. It can be examined by the natural sciences
and has been interpreted biblically and theologically in various ways.
Among these interpretations, we can find much upon which to base
our practice of discernment.

RECLAIMING THE BIBLICAL TRADITION ON NATURE

Even as we seek a renewed sense of nature, Christians must face the
charge that they have contributed to the destruction and commodifica-
tion of nature by interpreting literally the Genesis injunction to subdue
the earth and have dominion over all living creatures. "Dominion" has
usually been taken to mean domination over rather than governance for
the well-being of all living beings. The relevant question is: are humans
"over" nature or "in" nature? Clearly, Genesis shows humans embedded
in nature; they are thoroughly "of the earth" as the name Adam suggests
(*adamah*). At the same time, humans can enter into personal communion with God, and alone are spoken of as "created in the image of God"
in the first creation account. As beings who are both embedded in earth
and transcend earth, God gives humans a unique responsibility: to keep
order and peace between humans and the other creatures. God originally gave humans nonanimal foods, suggesting that God did not
intend humans to kill animals. Humans failed badly in this governing,
in keeping peace among creatures, so that, at the time of Noah, God
saw all the violence and "was sorry that he had made humankind." After
Noah, humankind ceased to be God's peacemaker with animals. God
delivers the animals to humans, who are allowed to kill them for self-
protection and for food. But this change of strategy on God's part only

underlines the fact that God's original intent was that there should not have been any killing of animals.[15]

Christians have also been prone to see the Old Testament as a chronicle of God's acts in history, so that nature becomes nothing more than a stage upon which God and humans act. But other metaphors for the relationship between God, humans, and nature are equally rooted in the Old Testament canon, and can ground a richer understanding of God and humans with and in nature. Two such metaphors that thread their way through the Old Testament are migration to a new land and fecundity.

In Deuteronomy, for example, land—the promised land to which the Hebrews migrated—is regarded as pure gift that Yahweh alone provides. Alongside the gratuitous gift of land is its sheer fecundity; it is "flowing with milk and honey."

> For the LORD your God is bringing you into a good land, a land with flowing streams, with springs and underground waters welling up in valleys and hills, a land of wheat and barley, of vines and fig trees and pomegranates, a land of olive trees and honey, a land where you may eat bread without scarcity, where you will lack nothing, a land whose stones are iron and from whose hills you may mine copper. You shall eat your fill and bless the LORD your God for the good land that he has given you.
>
> (Deut. 8:7–10)

As Yahweh fed the people in the desert through a sufficiency of food from the heavens, now Yahweh will feed the people through the more constant and stable gift of rich, fertile land to support them and their descendants. They look forward to wholesome harvests and the full cycle of the earth, all under the watchful and protective eyes of Yahweh, says Santmire, noting that this view of Yahweh is all the more striking because it is rooted in the north kingdom, where worship of Baal, the local deity of natural cycles, was much stronger than in the southern kingdom. Yahweh, the Lord of both nature and history, outdoes Baal at Baal's own game. This Lord works his will majestically in the Reed Sea and manifests himself with great glory at Sinai and throughout the earth.[16]

Many psalms likewise depict the universal reign of Yahweh. Others show God's care for all creatures. Even nature "understands" this unique relationship to the creator and so praises Yahweh:

> Praise him, sun and moon;
>   praise him, all you shining stars!

Praise him, you highest heavens,
    and you waters above the heavens! . . .
Praise the LORD from the earth,
    you sea monsters and all deeps,
fire and hail, snow and frost,
    stormy wind fulfilling his command!
Mountains and all hills,
    fruit trees and all cedars!
Wild animals and all cattle,
    creeping things and flying birds!
               (Ps. 148:3–4, 7–10)

The apocalyptic literature picks up the fecundity theme prevalent in Deuteronomy, carrying it into a time in which the people felt that the vision God had given them of secure land was no longer concretely realizable. Beginning with Third Isaiah, apocalyptic writers begin to lift up a still larger hope of an entirely new heaven and earth, a new day when Yahweh will make all things new. In this day, even our bodies shall flourish like grass (Isa. 66:14). The *Abba* of Jesus knows when the least sparrow falls (Matt. 10:29) and when all creation will be brought to its final fulfillment (Matt. 24:36). Paul articulates this theme in full-blown form in Romans 8, anticipating the day of the new heavens and the new earth:[17]

> For the creation waits with eager longing for the revealing of the children of God; for the creation was subjected to futility, not of its own will but by the will of the one who subjected it, in hope that the creation itself will be set free from its bondage to decay and will obtain the freedom of the glory of the children of God.
>
>   (Rom. 8:19–21)

The fecundity motif culminates in the Colossians and Ephesians. The cultural world of these texts is quite different from the apocalyptic world, which saw salvation in terms of time. The first-century world of Colossians and Ephesians saw fulfillment in terms of space. Reality is a towering and overlapping of dimensions extending from the earth upward through many layers of "powers" and "angels" to the highest of heavens. The rent in the unity of heaven and earth will be healed by the divine Redeemer filling all things with the Redeemer's salvific power, cosmic in scope. It encompasses all things. In these letters, the immanent power of God that unites heaven and earth is identified as Christ:[18]

He is the image of the invisible God, the firstborn of all creation; for in him all things in heaven and on earth were created, things visible and invisible, whether thrones or dominions or rulers or powers— all things have been created through him and for him. He himself is before all things, and in him all things hold together. He is the head of the body, the church; he is the beginning, the firstborn from the dead, so that he might come to have first place in everything. For in him all the fullness of God was pleased to dwell, and through him God was pleased to reconcile to himself all things, whether on earth or in heaven, by making peace through the blood of his cross.

(Col. 1:15–20)

NATURE IN CHRISTIAN THEOLOGY

Christian theology, while often ambivalent about nature, has not neglected it. Irenaeus, Augustine, and Calvin, to name three figures, each clearly articulated a theology that honors creation in its own right.

Earliest among them was Irenaeus (ca. 125–202), whose theology developed in response to the gnostics in and outside the Christian community who believed that they held special knowledge that separated them from common persons and that led to salvation. Irenaeus steadfastly opposed the gnostic rejection of the Creator God as well as their alternative: a passive, utterly removed deity. To Irenaeus, the Scriptures presented nature as humanity's God-given home; God brings the whole creation into being and will bring it to final fulfillment. In the center of this grand sweep of cosmic history, Irenaeus placed the Incarnate Word. This Word is both the eternal Logos who, with the spirit of God, is the ever-present life principle of creation history and, as the Word become flesh, moves the creation toward the final divine intention for creation. Embedded in Irenaeus's writings is the theme of migration to a good land, which is the renewed earth of the Creator of all things, not some heaven in the sky reserved for disembodied spirits. The God who one day will bless all things even now blesses them. Santmire concludes, "Irenaeus's theology, at its deepest levels, is an exposition of what can be called creation history."[19]

Augustine is widely perceived as a significant contributor to the hierarchical division between spirit and nature through his writings about fall and original sin. But in his middle and later years, Augustine became much more positively disposed to the created order. In *City of God*, he moved richly into the theme of migration to a new land.[20] Creation for Augustine is a manifestation of the goodness of God; through it we can contemplate God and God's providence, an important foundation and entry point for discernment:

> Ask the loveliness of the earth, ask the loveliness of the sea, ask the loveliness of the wide airy spaces, ask the loveliness of the sky, ask the order of the stars, ask the sun making the daylight with its beams, ask the moon tempering the darkness of the night that follows, ask the living things which move in the waters, which tarry on the land, which fly in the air; ask the souls that are hidden, the bodies that are perceptive; the visible things which must be governed, the invisible things that govern—ask these things, and they will all answer you, Yes, see we are lovely. Their loveliness is their confession. And all these lovely but mutable things, who has made them, but Beauty immutable.[21]

This passage clearly underlines the revelatory power of the beauties of nature, but it leaves unaddressed the violence of nature. Augustine was adamant that violence is not the result of the fall. The creation as a whole is not fallen; only that part of creation that has been touched by human sinfulness is fallen.

John Calvin went further, believing that the disorder perpetrated by sin did invade the elements of creation. These disorders are real, and they parallel the disorders in history. But God is still true to creation, bringing it to fulfillment. Creation is therefore to be enjoyed. It is a legitimate sphere in which Christians are to act, study, and exercise their considerable talents.[22] Furthermore, Calvin argued, we should not quickly move from contemplating nature to contemplating God, but we should instead "ponder them at length, turn them over in our minds seriously and faithfully, and recollect them repeatedly."[23]

While much of Christian theology and spirituality does focus on spirits ascending into heaven, leaving the natural world as the stage upon which human action takes place while on earth, we can find, as in these three figures, other biblical and theological treatments of nature upon which to lean as we turn to nature as an entry point for discernment.

HUMANS AS CREATED CO-CREATORS

Our journey to reclaim nature for discernment has one more stop. How might we think about human creativity in light of God's creativity? Is God the single creative agent, or do we also exercise creativity? Might there be a way to understand the relationship of divine and human creativity that would allow us to believe that the actions proceeding from our discernment are indeed a continuation of God's creative design for the world? Cultural biologist Philip Hefner speaks of humans as "created co-creators,"[24] extending an image that we first discussed in chapter 2. This image holds in tension, on one hand, human dependence on God as Creator—humans are fully creatures—and, on the other hand, free will—humans also shape their environment, making a genuine difference in the circumstances around them. How we use this ability to create, and that we do so in alignment with our Creator, is precisely the goal of discernment. We are simultaneously creatures and also partners with God in God's ongoing creation.

We have now completed seven entry points to discernment. It is possible that, after praying with three or four entry points, you began to get a sense of your tentative decision. If the additional ones continued toward the same decision, you have already begun the process of confirmation. The final chapter's exercises assist you in formalizing this crucial aspect of discernment.

11

Confirming One's Tentative Decision

The discernment journey you began when you carefully and prayerfully formulated your issue is finally coming to an end. You have prayed consistently for the spiritual freedom to follow God's call as it comes to you in the context of your decision. You gathered the data you need to make a sound decision, and chose from the seven entry points several that seemed the most useful, given your personality and the kind of issue you are discerning. You prayerfully considered what came through these entry points and eventually formulated a tentative decision.

Two more discernment steps remain: seeking confirmation and assessing the process. This chapter leads you in those two tasks. We learn what confirmation means, what a touchstone is, the biblical and spiritual heritage from which the touchstones spring, and how the fruit of the Spirit plays a part in confirmation. The four exercises begin with the prayer for confirmation, the heart of the chapter. The second exercise reviews and assesses the discernment process—the final step in discernment—and the third helps you prayerfully begin implementing your discerned decision. The final exercise, the Awareness Examen, reprises the first exercise in the book and carries you into the time between discernments.

Practice: Allowing God to Confirm a Discerned Decision

Before finalizing your decision, wait an amount of time that is reasonable given the seriousness of the decision (for example, overnight, a week, a month; the more significant the decision, the longer the time). During

---

this time, prayerfully review and test your tentative decision, using the following exercise one or more times. Your tentative decision is "confirmed" if, as you ponder it before God, you continue to experience it as the right decision or the best one for this moment.

1. Since you are seeking to follow God by means of this decision, recall and renew your desire to follow God's call as it is being worked out in this decision. Do not rush on to the next steps, but relish this prayer for spiritual freedom.

2. Prayerfully review all your discernment notes. What stands out from the perspective of the end of the process?

3. Ponder the following questions. They serve as markers to help you hold your decision up to the wisdom gleaned from the rich discernment tradition. Look for confirmation through the accumulation of positive indicators rather than any single one.

> Does the decision continue to sit well?
>
> Do you deeply desire this outcome?
>
> Does the consolation remain?
>
> Is the decision in accord with the biblical witness?
>
> Does your decision further and strengthen your personal commitments, for example, to family?
>
> Do others who know you well confirm your decision?
>
> Do other "fruit of the Spirit" (Gal. 5:22) appear in your life?
>
> Do you have the energy and necessary courage to proceed?

4. If your prayer and reflection raise new questions or doubts about your decision, return to earlier parts of the discernment process and repeat all or parts of the discernment. If, upon repeating, no clarity about moving ahead with the decision emerges, lay aside this outcome as not an expression of God's call for you at this time.

5. If the touchstones point toward affirmation, finalize the decision and give thanks to God.

THE FINAL STEPS

To the church member described in the introduction who wondered if discernment was some New Age invention, you can now say, "No!" It is neither esoteric knowledge, nor magic, nor New Age eclecticism. It is prayerfully seeking God with long and deep precedents in the biblical and spiritual tradition. Nor is it a completely different world from decision making that anyone might do. Chief executive officers who know nothing about discernment discover the issue about which a decision is needed; gather the necessary facts, data, and projections; consult the appropriate persons; weigh everything; and make a decision. They evaluate the decision after the fact and modify it if the results so indicate. Our discernment process has included all those steps; discernment appreciates and participates in the common wisdom about good decision making.

But those CEOs probably did not see decision making as a potential spiritual practice; most do not seek God's call in the decision, pray for spiritual freedom, or seek confirmation before finalizing the decision. Business leaders learn quickly that the bottom line is affected by the skill and the speed with which they can analyze, decide, and implement. The quicker they can move from decision to implementation, the more successful the decision is likely to be. In discernment, however, the opposite holds. Between making a tentative decision and the actual decision comes one of the important discernment distinctives, a process called confirmation. Once again, Ignatius of Loyola is the exemplar: "When the choice has been made, the person who has made it ought with great diligence to go to prayer before God our Lord, to offer him that choice, and to beg his Divine Majesty to receive and confirm it provided it is to his greater service and praise."[1]

The *Spiritual Exercises*, from which this point is taken, do not indicate what Ignatius means when he says that God would "confirm" the decision that we bring in earnest prayer. Fortunately, however, a small piece of Ignatius's journals survived, and it demonstrates Ignatius's practice with respect to confirmation. His discernment so far had led him to the tentative choice that the Society of Jesus should have no fixed sources of revenue as part of its practice of the vow of poverty. The fragment begins during the time Ignatius was trying to receive confirmation for this decision. Over successive days, we see him reviewing this choice, its parts and probable outcomes, and noticing what happens within him as he does so. He uses the inner barometer of consolation and desolation and watches any changes over a period of time, waiting for an unbroken time of consolation. We see him seemingly ready to conclude more than once, only to review the matter again. Finally, Ignatius realized that perfect certainty would not be possible, nor would unbroken consolation occur—that, in fact, he was trying to get God's confirmation in the way he would prefer rather than how God was extending it. Once he realized that prolonging his confirmation was more about his need for certainty than it was about God's confirmation, he promptly concluded the discernment.[2]

This snippet of Ignatius's journal helps us in several important ways to understand this crucial part of discernment. From his experience, we see not only that confirmation is a period of prayer in which we offer our discernment to God to receive and approve, but also that what comes to us as a result of this prayer will provide only relative certainty about our decision. Ignatius teaches us from this particular experience that it is only necessary to wait and pray for a reasonable amount of time, taking into account the complexity of the decision and the amount of time available. Ignatian scholar Michael Ivens writes, "We pray for confirmation in order to be as sure of doing God's will as it is given us to be and to counter the tendency in us to opt for hasty closure. . . . Confirmation can simply be that nothing comes up to call our decision into question."[3]

We also see that Ignatius used comparison to evaluate his tentative decision. He kept touching his tentative decision up against his experience of consolation and desolation, assuming that the Holy Spirit was most likely behind the consolation but not the desolation. As his experience of consolation and desolation shifted, his sense of clarity about how God was calling him did as well. But consolation and desolation are not the only wisdom that the tradition gives us to help us sense whether we are following the promptings of the Holy Spirit. We have already noticed some of this wisdom in chapter 9: Origen taught us that we should be suspicious if we feel compelled to act—for the Holy Spirit is found in growing inner freedom. Athanasius taught us that the Holy Spirit comes softly and quietly, causing strength, calmness of thought, joy, and settledness.

I call such bits of wisdom "touchstones" because we can touch our experience up against them in order to derive a sense about whether our direction is one to which God is calling us. Confirmation is simply prayerfully holding up our tentative decision to see how it fares when it is compared to—touched up against—the wisdom of the tradition. If the preponderance of the touchstones suggests that the Holy Spirit is indeed in our decision, and none of the touchstones raise a major caution, we can go ahead with confidence that God will be with us as we proceed. The questions you pondered in the exercise introduce you to the most significant of these biblical and traditional touchstones.

TOUCHSTONES IN THE TRADITION

Ignatius tended to use the presence of consolation as a strong indicator that God is confirming our decision. But he also encouraged the use of reason, advising that we ask, is this tentative decision for God's greater glory? What other touchstones might we find in the tradition? It turns out that there are a significant number.

Let's begin with Matthew's Gospel, near the conclusion of the Sermon on the Mount. Revisiting the question first asked much earlier in Israel's history, namely, how to discern true from false prophets, Matthew's Jesus gives his criteria: "You will know them by their fruits" (Matt. 7:16); the fruit of the prophet's life can be used to judge his prophecy. Using this text as a touchstone, we can look at the fruit in our own lives and those of others that has come about during our time of discernment and that we anticipate occurring as a result of the decision. Does this fruit suggest we are coming closer to God?

Paul gives us more help in his Letter to the Galatians. As the fifth chapter begins, he launches into an exhortation to live in freedom, claiming resoundingly, "For freedom Christ has set us free" (5:1). Using the touchstone of freedom, we can ask if our proposed decision flows from spiritual freedom and leads to an increase in it, as Origen also believed it should. In describing how the Spirit is manifest, Paul generates two lists; after he describes the fruit of the "flesh" he offers a list of fruit of the Spirit: "By contrast, the fruit of the Spirit is love, joy, peace, patience, kindness, generosity, faithfulness, gentleness, and self-control. There is no law against such things" (Gal. 5:22–23).

Notice the singular verb: the fruit of the Spirit *is*. The fruit of the Spirit is love. We also know the centrality of love from 1 Corinthians 13, Paul's paean to love. The fruit of the Spirit is joy. Pierre Teilhard de Chardin is credited with saying, "Joy is the infallible sign of God's life in us." The fruit of the Spirit is peace, *shalom*. The list is typical. Paul could have listed other virtues—courage, for example. When the Quakers, whom we met in chapter 5, sought confirmation they looked for such fruits as soberness, stillness, strength, unity, grace, and good order, as well as Paul's more familiar list.

But beware, for the virtues in Paul's list can also be counterfeited. Is the peace you feel actually the *shalom* that marks the Holy Spirit, or is it a false and shallow imitation, perhaps relief that a decision has been made? Does your patience come from the Spirit's perseverance, or is it really apathy disguised as patience? The fruit of the Spirit, as all the touchstones, must be discerned. Taking our cue from the singular verb that Paul employs, we should look for an increase of several, indeed most, of the virtues *simultaneously*. The variety of names for the ripples of the Spirit's action, held together, will help us avoid reifying or misdi-agnosing any single one. Are we more loving *and* more joyful *and* more kind and gentle all together?

Matthew also offers another touchstone in the Beatitudes. Blessed, he says, are the poor of spirit, the meek, those who hunger and thirst for justice, the merciful, the peacemakers, and those who suffer persecution for righteousness' sake. These, too, are signs of the growth of the life of the Spirit, so that if we grow in these qualities as a result of our decision, we can rest in our decision as the call of God.

We'll look at some of the Johannine touchstones later, seeing them through the eyes of the great Puritan theologian Jonathan Edwards. First, let's turn to the contribution of the Acts of the Apostles, where we see the power of the Holy Spirit in the community, bringing it to unity and fruitfulness. The new followers of the Way share their goods, care for those most needy among them, preach the gospel, and practice the breaking of bread and prayers. Do similar actions appear or grow as a result of our discernment?

The work of patristic authors, reflecting and synthesizing the biblical precedents, is rich with discernment material, and we can cull several important touchstones from this period to add to those of Origen and Athanasius. In the second century, Irenaeus of Lyons famously said, "The glory of God is the human being fully alive."[4] Do the decisions we have discerned bring more life? Do our deep desires point us toward these decisions? John Cassian (360–435) spoke of humility and open-ness of heart as characteristic of the Spirit's action.[5] Have we grown in true humility and genuine openness through this process?

Our necessarily brief overview jumps ahead to the Religious Society of Friends (Quakers). Quaker wisdom suggests that we are less likely to be doing our own will if what we are called to entails some level of suf-fering with Christ. They give fine examples of bringing one's discernment to the larger community for its response and endorsement as a means of protecting against self-delusion. The principle of "God Within," so central to George Fox, founder of the Quakers, produces soberness, peace, stillness, quietness, and strength, which Friends usually summarize as "the presence of inner peace."[6] Does Quaker wisdom give us any clarity about our tentative decision? Have others who know us well confirmed that we are on the right track? Do we experience the presence of inner peace?

Arguably the most important modern Reformed voice on discernment is Jonathan Edwards. In *Distinguishing Marks of a Work of the Spirit of God*, Edwards suggests that the presence of certain signs appearing in our life can help us recognize the saving work of the Holy Spirit. These "reliable signs," which are based on the First Letter of John, include:

1. The decision raises the esteem of Jesus and the truth of the gospel concerning him (1 John 4:2–3).
2. The spirit operates against the interests of Satan's kingdom (1 John 4:4–5).
3. The decision causes a greater regard for the Holy Scriptures, and establishes them more in their truth and divinity (1 John 4:6).
4. The decision operates as a spirit of truth, leading persons to truth, convincing them of those things that are true (1 John 4:6).
5. The decision manifests love of God and of other persons, winning and drawing the heart with those motives and enticements to love, giving a spirit of peace and goodwill, and it excites to acts of outward kindness (1 John 4:7, 12–13).[7]

So we can check our tentative decision against this wisdom: Is our love of Jesus and the truth of the gospel growing? our esteem for the Scriptures? our love of truth? Do we manifest more goodwill and greater peace?

In the second of Edwards's major treatises on discernment, *Religious Affections*, we find another set of touchstones, but here he is interested in the inner personal signs that reveal the saving work of God. He offers twelve such signs: a divine and supernatural source; attraction to God and God's ways for their own sake; seeing the beauty of holiness; a new knowing about spiritual things; deep-seated conviction; humility; a true change of nature; a Christlike spirit; a softened heart and tenderness of spirit; balance; hunger for God; and growth in Christian practices.[8] Edwards's signs give us more touchstones: Are we more attracted to God and the ways of God? Is that attraction resulting in better balance? Is it manifested in desire for God, or humility, or deep conviction about what is right? Do these inner sentiments actually lead to growth in Christian practices? Such signs indicate our decision is leading us toward God.

USING THE TRADITION APPROPRIATELY

This brief overview suggests that the long tradition contains much wisdom to help us judge the fruit of our discernment. Our ancestors gleaned this wisdom by reflecting on their own experience of God. They put what they learned into language that made sense to their contemporaries. But keep in mind that all of this wisdom is partial, conditional, and addressed to persons and communities very different from our own. It could have been presented in other words at other times and in other places. Are there touchstones in your own experience of God, moments when you are sure God was present and acting and against which you can touch your present experience? How has God been working in your particular community of faith? What does this suggest about how God is working in your decision now?

The Christian tradition has also garnered wisdom about how to use touchstones. Not every touchstone will be present in any single discernment. Some touchstones may even be contradicted. We look only for a preponderance of positive indicators and a minimum of negative indicators, but we must pay close attention to those touchstones that seem to be contradicted. For example, one of the touchstones in Allowing God to Confirm a Discerned Decision suggests that a fruitful decision will strengthen our previous commitments. It is possible, of course, to imagine times when God might be calling us out of a previous commitment. If this seems to be the case for you, then be doubly certain that other indicators are strong enough to suggest that you can overlook this important indicator. Do others, for example, agree that God seems to be calling you out of your commitment into something new?

If you carefully discern a decision, pray for and receive confirmation, and implement it, only to have it turn out badly, have you failed to discern or discerned badly? Not necessarily, for decision and discernment are not identical. Discernment is seeking God in the context of a decision. Our hypothetical CEO might have fine decision-making abilities but lack discernment. Because discernment and decision making are distinct, it is also possible that your decision making can be faulty or limited, and yet you will have nonetheless sought God's call to the best of your ability. Perhaps you lacked an important piece of data or based your conclusion on a faulty premise. Perhaps the situation changed without your knowledge, or another person's decision set in motion a series of events that derailed your decision. If you have sincerely sought God's call, you can trust that God will be with you as you try to repair the results of less-than-perfect decisions.

But the news is even better than that! Isaiah tells us that even if we would turn our backs on God in defiance, God will still lead us and repay us with comfort.

> Because of their wicked covetousness I was angry;
>   I struck them, I hid and was angry;
>   but they kept turning back to their own ways.
> I have seen their ways, but I will heal them;
>   I will lead them and repay them with comfort.
>   (Isa. 57:17–18)

But if God is with us through good and bad decisions, why go to the trouble to discern? Because discernment is the practice of seeking God in the midst of our daily lives, through all that happens to us. Decision making is one of the most human of activities. Since decisions are so significant in making us who we are, should we not seek God in the very act of deciding? What more powerful place to focus a spiritual practice than in the midst of a decision?

LEARNING DISCERNMENT FROM DISCERNING

Nonetheless, we'd like to make good decisions and become more skillful and faithful in our discernment. The final step in the discernment process, taking a look back, is shared with all good decision making, and

---

Practice: Reviewing and Evaluating Discernment

1. Ask God for the grace to see ever more clearly, follow God more nearly, and love God more dearly.

2. Look back over all the steps of your discernment. First, notice how

you proceeded through the various steps. Which steps, if any, did you omit, and what difference might including these steps have made in your discernment? Note how the steps built upon one another, checking for continuity.

3. Recall your own internal state as you discerned: Did you allow your desire to follow God's call to lead, or were you inclined to want God to follow you where *you* wanted to go? What moments stand out as particularly fruitful or full of consolation? If you notice a place where you went off track, what can you now learn from it so that your next discernment will have more integrity?

4. Now look back at the fruit of your decision. Over time, what has happened? Does any part of the decision need to be adjusted or revisited? What graces have come from the decision as it plays out?

5. Thank God that God goes with you.

can help us do just that. Even if we discover flaws in our process or lack of generosity in our response, we can gain invaluable knowledge for our future discernments.

Ignatius of Loyola is the source of this practice. In his second set of "Rules for Discernment of Spirits," in which the discerner learns about very subtle ways the evil one can disrupt or dislodge the discernment process, Ignatius says:

> When the enemy of human nature has been perceived and recognized by his serpent's tail and the evil end to which he is leading, a new procedure becomes profitable for the person who was tempted in this way. He or she should examine immediately the whole train of the good thoughts which the evil spirit brought to the soul, including their beginning, and then how little by little the evil spirit endeavored to bring the soul down from the sweetness and spiritual joy in which it had been, and finally brought it to his evil intention. Thus the person, by understanding this experience and taking note of it, can be on guard in the future against the characteristic snares.[9]

According to Ignatius, we can learn about our discernment and about the ways we get tempted even when we have succumbed to the temptation.

This "discernment in reverse," this looking back and seeing what happened, means that nothing need be lost, even if we botch the discernment.

Notice the two levels to the review. The first concerns the process itself, as suggested by Ignatius. The second continues the process of confirmation, this time adding two new dimensions. The decision has been made and implemented. The situation is no longer hypothetical. Deciding and acting set loose new dynamics. Acting invites responses from others. We are, in fact, in a new discernment situation. Does this new discernment situation suggest that the original decision ought to be changed or tweaked? Or does it further confirm the original decision by the fruit that is appearing?

An important caution: a well-discerned decision should not be lightly or easily changed, and then only by again discerning. Why? Because there will always be resistance to any course of action. Sometimes we have "buyer's remorse" with our decisions and get cold feet as we set about their implementation. Sometimes others punish us for the decision, trying to get us to reverse course. If the spiritual masters are to be believed, we should expect such static around decisions, especially significant ones.[10]

We can help ourselves by preparing for the implementation of our decision, especially when it is likely to stir up resistance from within or without. The following exercise can help you pray about and put in place some supports before you carry out your decision.

Practice: Getting Ready to Implement

1. Seek God's wisdom in working out the practicalities around your decision.

2. Examine the decision you have just made. Ask:

— Can my decision be broken down into discrete steps? If so, note an appropriate order.
— Does anyone need to be informed about this decision in advance of its implementation? If so, what is the best way to do that?
— Who besides me might be involved in carrying out the decision? How will I invite them to this role?
— If some of them choose not to join me, what will I do?

3. Who will support you along the way?

4. If reflecting and praying on these practicalities elicits some fear or resistance, weigh that fear against your experience of spiritual freedom that resulted from your decision. Ask for the grace to act from that place of spiritual freedom.

Your discernment process is complete. When you begin to act on the outcome that emerges from your discernment, you will be doing it from a new situation that calls for a new question, new data, renewed prayer for spiritual freedom, and more waiting to hear God's call for that question in that moment. As you repeat this cycle, you become more and more attuned to listening for God's voice as it comes to you in the circumstances of daily life. You become a person of discernment.

We end where we began, with the Awareness Examen. Through regular practice of the examen, you have the opportunity to say yes to God's invitation in the ebb and flow of daily activities. You'll become progressively clearer about your actions and how they affect other people, better able to find God in all things, and will learn daily, even hourly, to act from increasing spiritual freedom. Says one who has prayed the examen for many years:

> The examen is like a mini-retreat. It helps me to remember what is important. It helps me to get my priorities realigned. Through the examen, I remember the important things; that I'm loveable, that God loves me, that God loved me into creation. I remember the whole point of why I am here: for God's, my own, and others' happiness. Then I can act out of this awareness during the day.[11]

There is no better way to carry the effects of our discernment more completely into our lives. In the times between more formal discernment processes, the Awareness Examen can keep your discernment alive and growing, as if you are breathing your discernment day by day.

LAST WORDS

You have learned about the characteristics of discernment when it occurs in the context of decision making. You have visited various entry points, and have, I hope, noticed how different the discernment prayer can be

Awareness Examen[12]

There are many versions of the Awareness Examen. This one differs somewhat in language and style from the version in chapter 1; use whichever version you find most helpful. This spiritual exercise is usually done in the evening, looking over the day, but you may use it to review with God any period of time or activity.

1. Slow down. Prepare yourself to pray by becoming aware of the love with which God looks on you.

2. Note the gifts God has given you today. Give thanks to God for them.

3. Ask God that this examen be a time of special grace and revelation.

4. With God, review the day. Look at the stirrings of your heart, your thoughts, and your choices as the day progressed. Which have been of God? Which not? What does God want to say to you about both?

5. Ask God for forgiveness for any failure or omission, and for healing from their effects.

6. Look forward to the following day, and plan concretely with God how to live it according to God's desire for your life.

---

depending on your entry point. I hope you have also discovered how God chooses to invite you into deeper relationship and discipleship.

As my final word, I invite you to make this process your own. A few guiding principles may help:

1. *Personalize it to your own way of making decisions.* Start with the process that uses your preferred way of deciding, but complement it with an entry point that elicits very different material or uses your least-preferred process, aware that God will work through each. By doing both, you will build on your strength, and also stave off the characteristic blindness of your preferred decision-making style. But more, you are inviting God into your least-preferred functions as well as the ones in which you shine.

2. *Personalize your discernment to the size of the decision before you.* In

major decisions, use many or all of the entry points; in minor decisions, move much more straightforwardly to a decision. Common sense can be very helpful here!

3. *Personalize your discernment to the time available.* The bigger the decision, the longer the time one would ideally allow for the discernment and confirmation. The smaller the decision, the briefer the time. As you become more accustomed to discernment, as it becomes more of a spiritual habit, the amount of time you need to discern will shorten. It is said of Ignatius of Loyola that he was constantly discerning, and that at times it took him only moments to have a sense of what would be more pleasing to God in a given situation. Rest assured, however, if you do not have time to complete every part of the process, do the best you can, make a decision, and proceed in the confidence that God is with you.

4. *Personalize your discernment to the circumstances of your life.* It is your life before God. God desires to be intimately involved in it. God desires you to become a discerning person. May it be so.

Notes

Introduction

1. Marjorie J. Thompson, *Soul Feast: An Invitation to the Christian Spiritual Life* (Louisville, KY: Westminster John Knox Press, 1995), x.

2. Cited in Walter Burghardt, "Contemplation," *Church* 5 (Winter 1989): 14–18.

Chapter 1

1. The italicized insert is adapted from the Daily Check-in used in the Spiritual Exercises in Everyday Life, Seattle, Washington.

2. Similar practices are called Consciousness Examen and Examination of Consciousness.

3. Timothy M. Gallagher, OMV, *The Examen Prayer: Ignatian Wisdom for Our Lives Today* (New York: Crossroad, 2006), 36.

4. As quoted in John Wronski, "The Ignatian Examen," PowerPoint presentation for SP4155 Spiritual Exercises in Context, Graduate Theological Union, Spring 2003.

5. David Longsdale, *Listening to the Music of the Spirit: The Art of Discernment* (Notre Dame, IN: Ave Maria Press, 1993), 47.

6. Luke T. Johnson, *Scripture and Discernment: Decision-Making in the Church* (Nashville: Abingdon, 1996), 110.

7. Joan Mueller, *Faithful Listening: Discernment in Everyday Life* (Kansas City: Sheed and Ward, 1996), 2.

8. Ibid.

9. Longsdale, *Listening*, 51.

10. Ibid., 59.

11. Ibid., 65.

12. Gordon T. Smith, *Listening to God in Times of Choice: The Art of Discerning God's Will* (Downers Grove, IL: InterVarsity Press, 1997), 26–41.

13. Ignatius of Loyola, *Spiritual Exercises*, trans. George E Ganss, in *Ignatius of Loyola: The Spiritual Exercises and Selected Works*, ed. George E. Ganss (New York: Paulist Press, 1991), no. 23.

14. Jacques Guillet, "Sacred Scripture," in *Discernment of Spirits*, trans. Innocentia Richards of the essay "Discernement des Esprits," from *Dictionnaire de Spiritualité ascetique et mystique* (Collegeville, MN: Liturgical Press, 1957), 17–24.

15. Ibid., 36.

16. Johnson, *Scripture and Discernment*, 62–64.

17. Guillet, "Sacred Scripture," 48–53.

18. Johnson, *Scripture and Discernment*, 78.

19. For a rich discussion of this process, along with prior discernments leading up to the gathering in Jerusalem, see ibid., chap. 5.

20. Ignatius of Loyola, *Spiritual Exercises*, no. 236.

21. Ibid., no. 235.

Chapter 2

1. John Calvin, *Institutes of the Christian Religion* 1.1.1; ed. John T. McNeill, trans. Ford Lewis Battles, LCC (Philadelphia: Westminster Press, 1960).

2. Ignatius of Loyola, *Spiritual Exercises*, no. 104.

3. Janet Ruffing, *Spiritual Direction: Beyond the Beginnings* (New York: Paulist Press, 2000), 12.

4. Philip Sheldrake, *Befriending Our Desires* (Notre Dame, IN: Ave Maria Press, 1994), 14.

5. Thomas Merton, *New Seeds of Contemplation* (London: Burns and Oates, 1961), 37.

6. Frederick Buechner, *Wishful Thinking: A Theological ABC* (New York: Harper & Row, 1973), 95. Buechner introduces this well-known quotation as follows: "By and large a good rule for finding out [what our vocation is] is this. The kind of work God usually calls you to is the kind of work (a) that you need most to do and (b) that the world most needs to have done. If you really get a kick out of your work, you've presumably met requirement (a) but if your work is writing TV deodorant commercials, the chances are you've missed requirement (b). On the other hand, if your work is being a doctor in a leper colony, you have probably met requirement (b), but if most of the time you're bored and depressed by it, the chances are you have not only bypassed (a) but probably aren't helping your patients much either."

7. Ruffing, *Spiritual Direction*, 15.

8. Ann Ulanov and Barry Ulanov, *Primary Speech: A Psychology of Prayer* (Atlanta: John Knox Press, 1982), 20.

9. Thomas Ryan, *Four Steps to Spiritual Freedom* (New York: Paulist Press, 2003), 243.

10. Pierre Wolff, *Discernment: The Art of Choosing Well* (Liguori, MO: Triumph Books, 1993), 68.

11. Ben Campbell Johnson, *Discerning God's Will* (Louisville, KY: Westminster/ John Knox Press, 1990), 19.

12. Beatrice Bruteau, *The Grand Option: Personal Transformation and a New Creation* (Notre Dame, IN: University of Notre Dame Press, 2001), 47, 140.

13. Ignatius of Loyola, *Autobiography*, trans. Parmananda Davarkar, in *Ignatius of Loyola: Spiritual Exercises and Selected Works*, ed. George E. Ganss (New York: Paulist Press, 1991), no. 14.

14. Ignatius of Loyola, *Spiritual Exercises*, no. 23.

15. Ibid.

16. Ryan, *Four Steps*, 1–15.

17. Bruteau, *Grand Option*, 61.

18. E. Edward Kinerk, "Eliciting Great Desires: Their Place in the Spirituality of the Society of Jesus," *Studies in the Spirituality of Jesuits* 16 (November 1984), 1–15.

19. See *Spiritual Exercises*, no. 23. Paraphrase by Sister Karen Doyle, cited in Ryan, *Four Steps*, 192.

Chapter 4

1. Miroslav Volf, *The End of Memory: Remembering Rightly in a Violent World* (Grand Rapids: Eerdmans, 2006), 25. Volf comments on the inevitable partiality of our memories, noting that, besides our limited perspective (we can only see from where we stand), we can only see one perspective at a time. Our memories can be enhanced if we can gather the perspective of others on the same event, and if we can reconstruct the stream of history in which the particular event occurred. The event and the actors in the event each have their own histories before and after the moment on which the memory focuses (50).

2. Graham Lindegger and Susan Rakoczy, "One Training Issue: The Psychological Competence of Spiritual Directors," *Presence* 3 (May 1997): 22.

3. Volf, throughout *The End of Memory*, treats extensively the difficulties in and imperative for the use of memory in a way that preserves the integrity of both the one remembering and the moral imperative to overcome evil with good.

4. This term is attributed to Reinhard Koselleck, but cited without further attribution in Volf, *End of Memory*, 101.

5. Joan D. Chittister, *Scarred by Struggle, Transformed by Hope* (Grand Rapids: Eerdmans, 2003), 102.

6. John Bunyan, *Grace Abounding*, ed. John Stachniewski with Anita Pacheco (Oxford: Oxford University Press, 1998), 4–5 (cited in Mark McIntosh, *Discernment and Truth: The Spirituality and Theology of Knowledge* [New York: Crossroad, 2004], 162).

7. For further resources on moments of freedom and touchstones for discernment,

see William Barry, SJ, *Letting God Come Close: An Approach to the Ignatian Spiritual Exercises* (Chicago: Loyola Press, 2001), 149–57.

Chapter 5

1. Ben Campbell Johnson, *Discerning God's Will* (Louisville, KY: Westminster/ John Knox Press, 1990), 69.

2. Cited at Oneira, "Dream Wisdom," http://koti.mbnet.fi/oneira.htm (accessed on July 25, 2005).

3. George M. Sauvage, "Intuition," in *The Catholic Encyclopedia,* online edition, 2003, transcribed by Tomas Hancil; cited at www.newadvent.org/cathen/ 08082b.htm (accessed on July 25, 2005).

4. An instrument for measuring a person's preferences, using four basic scales with opposite poles: (1) extraversion/introversion, (2) sensate/intuitive, (3) thinking/feeling, and (4) judging/perceiving. The various combinations of these preferences result in sixteen personality types, with extensive variations within these sixteen.

5. Paul D. Tieger and Barbara Barron-Tieger, "The Principles of Personality Type," in *The Art of Speed-Reading People,* chap. 1, cited at www.twbookmark.com/ books/63/0316845183/chapter_excerpt10245.html (accessed on July 26, 2005).

6. Sauvage, "Intuition."

7. Thomas Merton, *New Seeds of Contemplation,* (New York: New Directions, 1961), 267.

8. Ignatius of Loyola, *Autobiography,* 80–81.

9. Michael Sheeran, *Beyond Majority Rule: Voteless Decisions in the Religious Society of Friends* (Philadelphia: Philadelphia Yearly Meeting, 1983); Barry Crosno, The Quaker Dharma, "Intuition and Leadings," http://thequakerdharma.blogspot.com/ 2005/03/intuition-leadings.html (accessed on July 26, 2005).

10. Douglas V. Steere, ed., *Quaker Spirituality: Selected Writings* (New York: Paulist Press, 1984), 171.

11. Parker Palmer recounts being helped most in a clearness session about a new position he was considering by the question, "What color do you associate with each of these jobs, and why?" See "The Clearness Committee: A Way of Discernment," *Weavings* (July/August 1988): 37–40.

12. For descriptions of the Clearness Committee process, see Palmer, "The Clearness Committee"; Susanne Farnhand et al., *Listening Hearts: Discerning Call in Community,* rev. ed. (Harrisburg, PA: Morehouse, 1994), appendix 1: Guidelines for Discernment Groups; and Patricia Loring, "Spiritual Discernment," Pendle Hill Pamphlet (Wallingford, PA: Pendle Hill, 1992), no. 305.

Chapter 6

1. Stephanie Paulsell, *Honoring the Body: Meditations on a Christian Practice* (San Francisco: Jossey-Bass, 2002), 22–23.

2. Ibid., 15.

3. Ibid., 31.

4. Adapted from the version first published in John Endres and Elizabeth Liebert, *Praying the Psalms: Resources for Personal and Communal Prayer* (New York/Mahwah, NJ: Paulist Press, 2001), 180–82.

5. Eugene Gendlin, *Focusing: Second Edition with New, Revised Instructions* (New York: Bantam, 1981).

6. Peter A. Campbell and Edwin M. McMahon, *BioSpirituality: Focusing as a Way to Grow*, 2nd expanded ed. (Chicago: Loyola University Press, 1997).

7. Gendlin, *Focusing*, 10.

8. This adaptation is based on Gendlin, *Focusing*, 177–78, modified by the 2003 online version available at http://www.focusing.org/partnership/partner_info/short-forms.html. This site also contains versions developed by three other focusing experts. The Focusing Institute recommends downloading several versions and selecting the one that you find the most useful.

9. Stephen Mitchel, ed., *The Enlightened Heart* (New York: Harper & Row, 1988), 38–39, cited in Jane Vennard, *Praying with Body and Soul: A Way to Intimacy with God* (Minneapolis: Augsburg, 1998), 120–21.

Chapter 7

1. Johnson, *Discerning God's Will*, 81–85.

2. Peter Levitt, quoted by Andrew Beath in *Consciousness in Action: The Power of Beauty, Love, and Courage in a Violent Time* (New York: Lantern Books, 2005), 122.

3. Ray Hart, *Unfinished Man and the Imagination* (New York: Herder and Herder, 1968), 242; cited in Katherine Dyckman, Mary Garvin, and Elizabeth Liebert, *The Spiritual Exercises Reclaimed: Uncovering Liberating Possibilities for Women* (New York/Mahwah, NJ: Paulist Press, 2001), 122–23.

4. Dyckman, Garvin, and Liebert, *Spiritual Exercises Reclaimed*, 122–23.

5. E. Glenn Hinson, "The Progression of Grace: A Re-Reading of *The Pilgrim's Progress*," *Spiritus* 3, no. 2 (fall 2003): 257.

6. Deborah Smith Douglas, "To See with the Eyes of the Heart," *Weavings* 12, no. 1 (January/February 1997): 19–20.

7. Beath, *Consciousness in Action*, 84.

8. Johnson, *Discerning God's Will*, 89–92.

9. Elizabeth-Anne Vanek, *Image Guidance: A Tool for Spiritual Direction* (New York/Mahwah, NJ: Paulist Press, 1992), 25–27.

10. Adapted from ibid., 27–28.

11. Ibid., 25–27.

12. Wendy Wright, "Living into the Image: Thoughts on Religious Imagination and the Imagery of Tradition," *Weavings* 12, no. 1 (January/February 1997): 6–8.

13. Ignatius's own story of his conversion is given various titles: *Acts, Reminiscences,* and *Autobiography* being the most common. This part of his story is recounted in

paragraph numbers 5–8. A number of English translations exist; see, for example, Joseph Munitiz and Philip Endean, trans and eds., *Saint Ignatius of Loyola: Personal Writings* (New York: Penguin Books, 1996).

14. See Ignatius of Loyola, *Spiritual Exercises,* nos. 184–88.

Chapter 8

1. Ignatius of Loyola, *Spiritual Exercises*, no. 181.

2. Mark A. McIntosh, *Discernment and Truth: The Spirituality and Theology of Knowledge* (New York: Crossroad, 1994), 1–3.

3. Ibid., 217, 233.

4. Gordon Mursell, *English Spirituality: From Earliest Times to 1700* (London: SPCK; Louisville, KY: Westminster John Knox Press, 2001), 337.

5. McIntosh, *Discernment and Truth*, 12–23.

6. Evan Howard, *The Affirming Touch of God* (Lanham, MD: University Press of America, 2000), 102.

7. Jonathan Edwards, *The Religious Affections* (Carlisle, PA: The Banner of Truth Trust, 1961), 49–50.

8. Ibid., 192–93.

Chapter 9

1. I use "feelings" and "emotions" as synonyms, as in colloquial speech. It is possible to distinguish between them. For example, see Antonio R. Damasis, "Emotion in the Perspective of an Integrated Nervous System," *Brain Research Review* 26 (1998): 83–86. Damasis holds that since the limbic system is basically the same in animals and humans, we must conclude that emotions are not restricted to humans alone. He uses this conclusion to then distinguish the unconsciousness of emotions from the consciousness of feelings. Cited in Nancy J. Wiens, "Discernment and Nature: Exploring Their Relationship through Christian Spirituality and the Natural Sciences" (PhD dissertation, Graduate Theological Union, 2007), 206n70.

2. Kathleen Fischer, "Working with Emotions in Spiritual Direction: Seven Guiding Principles," *Presence: An International Journal of Spiritual Direction* 12, no. 3 (September 2006): 26–35.

3. Ibid., 26–27.

4. McIntosh, *Discernment and Truth*, 93.

5. Ibid., 94.

6. Ignatius of Loyola, *Spiritual Exercises*, no. 335.

7. Wolff, *Discernment*, 25.

8. Edwards, *Religious Affections*, 23.

9. Gerald McDermott, *Seeing God: Twelve Signs of True Spirituality* (Downers Grove, IL: InterVarsity Press, 1995), 31–33.

10. Edwards, *Religious Affections*, 23, 50.

11. Jules Toner, *A Commentary on Saint Ignatius' Rules for the Discernment of Spirits* (St. Louis: Institute of Jesuit Sources, 1982): 94–144. Cf. Ignatius of Loyola, *Spiritual Exercises,* nos. 316–17.

12. For thorough and accessible descriptions of consolation and desolation, see Timothy M. Gallagher, OMV, *The Discernment of Spirits: An Ignatian Guide for Everyday Living* (New York: Crossroad, 2005), esp. chaps. 3 and 4.

13. Ignatius of Loyola, *Spiritual Exercises*, no. 333.

Chapter 10

1. Sallie McFague, "Should a Christian Love Nature?" *The Spire* (*Vanderbilt University Divinity School and Oberlin Graduate School of Theology*) 15, no. 3 (spring–summer 1993): 1, 11–12.

2. H. Paul Santmire, *The Travail of Nature: The Ambiguous Ecological Promise of Christian Theology* (Minneapolis: Fortress Press, 1985), 9.

3. Mark I. Wallace, *Finding God in the Singing River: Christianity, Spirit and Nature* (Minneapolis: Fortress Press, 2005). While I do not agree with all of Wallace's constructive proposals, his attempt to combine Christian biblical and theological voices with Native American, Neo-Pagan, and philosophical voices to weave a rich tapestry of creative visioning about the relationship of Christianity and nature is compelling reading.

4. Beatrice Bruteau, *God's Ecstasy: The Creation of a Self-Creating World* (New York: Crossroad, 1997).

5. McFague, "Should a Christian Love Nature?" 1.

6. Wallace, *Finding God*, 45, italics his.

7. McFague, "Should a Christian Love Nature?" 3.

8. Quoted in Susan Brooks Thistlethwaite and Mary Potter Engle, eds., *Lift Every Voice* (San Francisco: HarperSanFrancisco, 1990), 3.

9. Mary Oliver, *Thirst* (Boston: Beacon Press, 2006), 37.

10. Adapted from Maria Harris, *Women and Teaching: Themes for a Spirituality of Pedagogy* (New York: Paulist Press, 1988), 41–42.

11. McIntosh, *Discernment and Truth*, 206.

12. Robert John Russell, "Contemplation: A Scientific Concept," *Continuum* (December 1990): 135–53.

13. Contemporary spirituality scholar Nancy Wiens, who is working on the interface between natural sciences, theology, and the practice of discernment, offers one way to clear up this constant confusion. She uses "Nature" to refer to all creatures including humans and "nature" to refer to all nonhuman creatures. See "Discernment and Nature: Exploring Their Relationship through Christian Spirituality and the Natural Sciences" (PhD dissertation, Graduate Theological Union, April 2007), 1–2n1. While I do not observe this custom here, it does give a way to preserve a distinction that is sometimes critical about the "situation" of humans with respect to the rest of creation.

14. Santmire, *Travail*, 11–12.

15. Annette Schellenberg, "'. . . and in the Image of God He created them . . .': P's concept of Man in Historical and Theological Perspective," San Francisco Theological Seminary, February 6, 2007, manuscript.

16. Santmire, *Travail*, 191, 194.

17. Ibid., 201–2, quotation on 201.

18. Ibid., 203–6.

19. Ibid., 35–49, quotation on 35.

20. Ibid., 56. See, for example, Augustine, *City of God*, 22:24.

21. Augustine, *Sermons*, 241:2, cited in Santmire, *Travail*, 66–67.

22. Susan E. Schreiner, *The Theatre of His Glory: Nature and the Natural Order in the Thought of John Calvin* (Grand Rapids: Baker Books, 1991), 121.

23. Calvin, *Institutes*, 1.14.21.

24. Philip Hefner, *The Human Factor: Evolution, Culture and Religion* (Minneapolis: Fortress Press, 1993), 147. Nancy Wiens introduced me to Hefner's notion of humans as created co-creators; she employs this image to summarize spiritual anthropology that undergirds her rethinking of the place of Nature in discernment. See Wiens, "Discernment and Nature," 244–45.

Chapter 11

1. Ignatius of Loyola, *Spiritual Exercises*, no. 183. I have translated "*elección*" as "choice," though many translators simply use the cognate "election." "Election" has thus taken on somewhat of a technical meaning and may, for our purposes, obscure the straightforward sense of this point.

2. Ignatius of Loyola, "Selections from *The Spiritual Diary*," in George Ganss, ed., *Ignatius of Loyola: Spiritual Exercises and Selected Works* (New York: Paulist Press, 1991), 238–70.

3. Michael Ivens, SJ, *Understanding the Spiritual Exercises: Text and Commentary: A Handbook for Retreat Directors* (Herefordshire, England: Gracewing, 1998), 141.

4. *Adversus Haereses*, 14.20.7: "For the glory of God is a living man; and the life of man consists in beholding God. For if the manifestation of God which is made by means of the creation affords life to all living in the earth, much more does that revelation of the Father which comes through the Word, give life to those who see God"; translation from New Advent, http://www.newadvent.org/fathers/0103420.htm (accessed February 19, 2007).

5. Gustave Bardy, "The Patristic Period," in "Discernment of Spirits," translation of the article "Discernement des Esprits" from the *Dictionnaire de Spiritualité Ascetique et Mystique*, vol. 111, cols. 1222–91, trans. Innocencia Richards (Collegeville, MN: Liturgical Press, 1957), 60.

6. Michael Sheeran, *Beyond Majority Rule: Voteless Decisions in the Religious Society of Friends* (Philadelphia: Philadelphia Yearly Meeting, 1983), 24–28.

7. Christian Classics Ethereal Library, http://www.ccel.org/ccel/edwards/works2.vii.htm (accessed on February 20, 2007).

8. These paraphrases of Edwards's much longer titles are adapted from McDermott, *Seeing God*, 232–33.

9. Ignatius of Loyola, *Spiritual Exercises*, no. 334.

10. See C. S. Lewis's *Screwtape Letters* for a classic tale of such resistance. For an Ignatian treatment of how this static gets kicked up, see Gallagher, *Discernment of Spirits,* esp. chaps. 1 and 2.

11. Cited in Gallagher, *Examen Prayer*, 160.

12. Adapted from ibid., 25.

Index of Scripture Citations